AFTER DINNER
SPEECHES AND STORIES

After Dinner Speeches and Stories

by

JOHN BOLTON

author of
"Modern Careers for Boys"

LONDON

W. FOULSHAM & CO. LTD.

NEW YORK : TORONTO : CAPE TOWN : SYDNEY

W. FOULSHAM & CO. LTD.,
Yeovil Road, Slough, Berks., England.

CONTENTS

Foreword

ANYONE who has ever attended a Dinner where After Dinner Speeches and Toasts have been the order of the day knows very well just what a difference a really good speaker making a first class speech can make.

All too often the After Dinner speaker is inarticulate, incomprehensible and much too long-winded. The diners are generally keen to get on with the rest of the evening's entertainment which is usually dancing, but which could be a smoking concert, a display of some sort or a cabaret and, at the best, the Speeches become merely a means of filling in the time while the company relaxes and digests its meal.

The good speaker knows how to make a witty, memorable speech; he knows how much to say, how to say it and when not to say it! He does not bore his listeners with long, wearisome anecdotes about himself and other people who are not known to the present company, nor does he use the After Dinner Speech to pay off old scores. Unlike the political platform, the After Dinner Speech is never heckled nor interrupted in any way, and the speaker who takes advantage of this fact by attacking an individual or a group who are prevented by good manners from replying, will probably not again be asked to speak at such a function.

To be a good After Dinner speaker is an asset that can be acquired by anybody willing to spend a small amount of time in the preparation of the speech and another amount of time in practising the speech. Very few people can make a good, impromptu speech and the beginner should certainly never try to do so.

In this book we have included all the aspects of speech-making at After Dinner functions—we explain in detail just how to prepare a speech, how to deliver it, some specimen speeches, some useful quotations and some good After Dinner stories which judicially introduced into a speech will bring humour and help to create an atmosphere of hilarity.

With regard to the specimen speeches. It is not intended that these should be used verbatim. There are very few occasions when it will be found that these specimens cover all the aspects of any one particular set of circumstances. They are intended to be used as a guide only, and would-be speakers should adapt them to their own special requirements.

Nor should the quotations be used indiscriminately. They should be interwoven with the fabric of the speech only if they are apt and to the point in connection with the main theme of the speech. These quotations, however, may set off a train of thought that will be helpful in the preparation of a speech and it is primarily for this purpose that they are intended.

The jokes too, should be used sparingly and always in context. They should not be dragged in merely for the sake of their humorous appeal. To tell a golfing story at the Golf Club's Annual Dinner will be appreciated, and you will acquire a reputation as a witty speaker; to use the same story at a Dinner given for a visiting celebrity will merely label you as being "rather stupid". Make full use of humour when the subject demands it, but make sure you are using the humour that fits the situation.

A final word of encouragement to the beginner about to make his first After Dinner Speech. Think of the best, wittiest, most popular After Dinner speaker that you know or have heard about and remember that he, too, once had to face an audience for the first time. Remember, too, that the company has probably dined and wined well and will be feeling in a mellow mood. Therefore, they will be very receptive and provided you have carefully prepared your speech as we have suggested you will find your audience very sympathetic.

CHAPTER ONE

Preparing the Speech

In preparing the speech you must consider both yourself and your audience. Remember that you have got to deliver the speech. You know your own ability of expression and you know your limitations. Make concessions to them. If it is your first speech do not be too ambitious but prepare instead a simple, modest kind of talk; full-blooded oratory and dramatic delivery is only succesful after much experience in the field of speech-making. Do not set yourself a task that is too great for you; it is no good composing a beautiful speech if it is too beautiful for you to deliver properly.

Consideration of your audience calls for a good deal of thought. Obviously there will be a considerable difference in style between a speech made at a Regimental Dinner and a speech given at an Old Girls Reunion Dinner. Naturally the subject determines the style to a certain extent, and you must consider what sort of persons there will be in your audience. Consider their age, their sex, their social status and especially their relationship to yourself. If you know most of them by their Christian names, don't speak to them as if they were all strangers. If you don't know any of them do not pretend that you do even by implication. Be sincere and do not speak with your tongue in your cheek. Do not say anything that you disbelieve because it will not ring true and an intelligent audience will not be fooled for one moment. Do not offend good taste by obtaining a cheap laugh at some one else's expense. Above all, bear in mind your audience when you are choosing any jokes or funny stories for inclusion in your speech. What may go down very well at a stag dinner could be very much out of place at a Ladies' Night Dinner.

Speeches are meant to be heard and not to be read. This may seem very obvious, but a really good speech cannot be prepared unless this fact is kept constantly in mind. To illustrate the truth of this, sit down one evening and listen— really *listen*—to a speech on the radio or television given by a reputed master of oratory. Doubtless you will be impressed and think what a fine speech this was, even if perhaps you were not in agreement with the subject matter. Then read the context of the speech in the daily paper or *The Listener* and see the difference. The written speech is lifeless, dull and uninteresting. It needed the personality and special delivery of the speaker to bring it to life and to give it warmth and interest.

To convince yourself even further try reading an interesting article which you have seen in a magazine or newspaper aloud. It was probably an enthralling article, but it sounds wrong somehow when it is delivered as a speech. So by now, you will have seen by practical application the vast difference between the notes written up for oral delivery, and the article written for publication.

Obviously then when you are preparing an After Dinner speech you should keep trying it out aloud to make sure that it *sounds* right.

In certain respects, however, good speeches and good articles have points in common. Both should be clear, not muddled; the arrangements of facts and arguments should be orderly and logical; there should be no waste of words or digressions; and the style should be simple and direct.

First stages in speech-making. You have been called upon to make an after dinner speech, to propose a toast or move a vote of thanks at a dinner given by your club or association, so how are you going to go about it?

The first thing to bear in mind is that whatever the nature of the toast it needs preparation in advance. Some people can get up and make an extempore speech without any preparation, but those who do this are usually persons who have had a lot of experience in public speaking. If you know in advance that you are going to be called on to make a speech, do not leave it till the last minute. Do not imagine that you will be able to rise to the occasion without having given it any thought beforehand. Do not delude yourself with the idea that "You'll think of something when the time comes". The chances are strongly against your doing any such thing. You will probably be tongue tied and stutter, and feel so absolutely miserable that you will probably decide never to make another speech ever again.

To start the preparations, choose a time when you can sit down quietly for about half an hour to consider the whole matter. Do not try to begin preparations for a speech during a hurried lunch-hour or while waiting for the water to boil when making a cup of tea. Sit down with a pencil and some scrap paper and really concentrate on the subject in hand.

First of all think of the subject about which you are to talk, decide what line you are going to follow and then start to jot down your ideas. In the first instance you will probably have several ideas, so write them all down. Then get them into order so that one sequence follows upon another. Cut out any irrelevancies or repetition and if your speech is to include any facts or statistics, check them here and now to make sure you have them correctly. Never take chances on proven facts or figures because you may be sure that someone in your audience will spot any mistake and once you are detected in error, you will find that there is an air of general disbelief covering your whole speech. "He (or she) has made one mistake" will be the obvious reaction of your audience "He has probably made many others!"

Now that you have marshalled your ideas and got them into some form of order try saying the speech out loud and testing it for smooth running and unobtrusive lead-ins from paragraph to paragraph and subject to subject. This is the stage when you will discover your own personal characteristics with regard to speech making. You will notice that you tend to put emphasis on certain words and on certain phrases. Sentences written down in your notes will just not lend themselves to being spoken aloud, and you will find yourself automatically correcting them as you go along. When this happens make pencil corrections to your jottings and keep on saying dubious phrases and sentences over and over again until they eventually "come right." Now you are ready to write your model speech. With the aid of your notes, corrections and amendments you can write out your entire speech in the way in which, more or less, you will deliver it on the night. You may find that your speech needs revision during the next day or so, for each time you read it over you will doubtless find some improvements to be made. In your search for perfection however, do not overdo the revision and pruning work. If you concentrate too much on your speech you may find it suddenly stales on you, and that the words become a meaningless jumble of nonsense. If this does happen, try to forget the speech for at least 24 hours, or as long as you possibly can; put it right away in a drawer somewhere and take a fresh look at it with an open mind.

Keep it brief! You rarely hear complaints about a speech being too short, but you do hear many complaints that a speech was too long. Most Dinners are followed by a cabaret and dancing, and the diners are naturally keen to get on with the enjoyment of the evening's festivities. They will not thank you for keeping them from these pleasures for an unnecessarily long, boring speech. If you are given a time limit, keep to it; if you are not given a time limit consider the length of time you yourself would be prepared to sit and listen to a speech such as you are planning to make, then knock a few minutes off and use that as your time limit. And remember that when you time yourself you must make liberal allowance for pauses and, it is sincerely to be hoped, for applause and laughter. It is better far to finish before your time than go rambling on beyond the time limit.

Prepare your speech in short sentences. They are easier to remember, easier to deliver and easier for your listeners to grasp. There is nothing so pathetic—or ridiculous—as hearing a speaker start a sentence and then lose the thread of it so that he does not know how to bring it to a finish. As a beginner try to stick to simple sentences consisting of subject, verb and predicate and keep away from involved dependent clauses. This may not be good style from a literary point of view, but it is the safest form of preparation for a speech. If you normally write in long sentences, split them up ruthlessly in the course of revision. Remember that you have got to say them and breathe! Any faults of this kind that you make in the preparation of the speech will come back on you when you commence delivery.

Do not use long words if you know shorter ones that mean the same thing. Do not say, for instance, "commence" instead of "begin" or "request" instead of "ask." Above all, do not use words which you do not properly understand.

Do not try to impress your audience by the use of ornate and pompous words or phrases. Those of the audience who do not understand will be irritated, and those who do understand them will think you pretentious.

By far the best plan is to use only words that you normally use in everyday conversation. If you are trying to use words that are not in your everyday vocabulary, you run the risk of using them incorrectly. We do not mean that a person should not have an extensive vocabulary; in fact a good grasp of the English language adds colour to a speech and helps the speaker to string together good resounding sentences without the need for over repetition, but do not keep one vocabulary for speeches and the other for day-to-day use. Try above all to be natural. If you adopt a pose, the audience will spot it immediately. Speak as you would in everyday conversation. Do not think that speech-making calls for a more "refined" or "educated" language. Making a speech is much the same as taking part in an everyday conversation; but instead of speaking to one or two people you are speaking to a number of persons at one time.

Do try too, to avoid the use of foreign phrases. Unless you can really speak the language from which the phrase is taken it will sound "phoney" and rather silly. If you cannot pronounce a phrase such as "savoire faire" properly, it is far better to use the English "know-how." Again, do not give foreign pronunciations to words which have become a part of the English language. Do not say "Continong" when you mean "Continent" or say "When I was travelling in España" when you mean "When I was travelling in Spain."

Steer clear of archaisms and clichés. The use of such words or phrases is an affectation. The whole reason why a word is dubbed "archaic" is because it is no longer used. And do not delude yourself or try to delude your audience with the excuse that there is no other word to express your meaning. There always is!

Typical archaisms, which some speakers will consistently include in their speeches are "behest," "perchance," "damsel," "yclept" and so on. They sound over-theatrical and ridiculous when applied to modern speech-making.

More difficult to achieve, but really equally important, is the avoidance of clichés. A cliché is an indirect way of expressing a simple idea which was probably striking when it was first used, but which has since become stale and over-worked by too frequent usage. In the course of time, too, such clichés become misquoted and used in the wrong context with the result that they often become meaningless.

The difficulty arises from the fact that clichés, like popular catchphrases (which should also be avoided) are over prevalent in our newspapers and in radio and television programmes. It may be argued that if a speech is to resemble conversation, then clichés ought to be permissible. The answer to this is that clichés are faults in all English, written or spoken, including conversation; and they are especially irritating when delivered in a public speech.

If you write out the first draft of your speech quickly—and you should do it quickly—then it will almost certainly contain several clichés. Never mind about them while you are writing, but go through the draft afterwards and weed them out.

Some of the commonest clichés which turn up with monotonous regularity in after dinner speeches are:

"Conspicuous by his absence"; "the cup that cheers but does not inebriate"; "washing our dirty linen in public"; "sleeping the sleep of the just"; "slowly but surely"; "kindly but firmly"; "more in sorrow than than in anger"; "the situation would be funny if it were not so tragic"; "like the curate's egg"; "leave well alone"; "maintaining the *status quo*"; "make haste slowly" and so on and so on.

All these and the thousands of other similar expressions were neat, shrewd or witty when they were first used. Now the novelty has worn off and they are merely tedious. If you can think of an effective and original way of expressing something, then use it. And perhaps one day, you will find it in a list of clichés.

The use of humour, quotations and slang. Humour is desirable in most after dinner speeches. The purpose of a Dinner is usually a light-hearted one—the Annual Dinner of a Sports' Club or some kind of Association, a Regimental Dinner, a Reunion Dinner, a Ladies Night, or a pleasant means of raising funds for some worth while project. Therefore the speeches should not be too heavy in tone. There may be need for a *serious* speech; you may be appealing for funds, deploring the drop in membership, or referring to some shortcoming on the part of the local Council. In such a case a lot of facetious comment would be out of place, but even so if you can start your speech with a joke or some humorous reference, you will immediately engage the attention of the audience and, if your speech has been well prepared, continue to hold their attention.

In introducing any form of humour into a speech there are several points to watch. First be sure that your jokes are in good taste and suitable to the present audience. If you have any doubt at all that a particular joke may give offence, then don't use it. Do not involve other people personally in your humour. When you know a person very well indeed it is sometimes permissible to pinpoint some characteristic or *trait* and weave it in humorously into your speech. But when you do this be absolutely certain in your mind that the person in the case is going to appreciate the joke and be able to laugh with you. That is the important point in personal humour. Do make quite certain that the victim is going to be able to laugh with the audience, not that the audience is going to laugh *at* anyone. The safest personal joke is the joke against yourself. When you are using a joke, whether it is one of the many examples given in this book, or one which you may have heard on radio or television, give it a new twist, do not repeat it word for word as you heard it or read it. Vary the wording a little to give it your own personal touch. Keep clear of puns, they are not popular. Above all, be sure your jokes have some bearing on the subject matter of your speech. If a joke has been "dragged in" or merely told for the sake of telling, it loses its point.

Humorous stories are valuable additions to most speeches, but they must observe these simple rules. A humorous story is simple to tell. It does not call for great oratory and you are likely to find it easier to be natural when you are telling a tale than when speaking more formally. But it must be in good taste; it should have a fresh appeal to the audience; and it must have sufficient bearing on your speech to justify its inclusion.

An apt quotation can also be very effective, but it must be *apt*. Do not quote too often, and do not use quotations to show how well read or well educated you may be. Avoid quotations in a foreign language, particularly in Latin or Greek (unless of course you are speaking to a gathering of University Dons or a similar body of erudite persons) because a lot of your audience will not understand a word of what you are saying and you will lost their attention. We have included a list of useful quotations in another chapter of this book, but it should be stressed that these are for guidance only and should only be used if they really will fit in with what you are going to say. A hackneyed quotation is as bad as a cliché. Such quotations as "to be or not to be" "trip the light fantastic toe" "once more into the breach" and other over used quotations should be avoided at all costs.

Whenever you do use a quotation, make sure that you have it correctly. "All that *glisters* is not gold" not "All that glitters is not gold"; "A little *learning* is a dangerous thing" not "A little knowledge is a dangerous thing"; "Fresh *woods* and pastures new" not "Fresh fields and pastures new"; "*Lay* on, MacDuff" not "Lead on, MacDuff". These are a few of the correct quotations which are so often mis-quoted in public speeches.

The use of slang depends to a great extent upon the nature of your audience. It can be used with great effect, but it must be used with restraint. Too much slang gives an over-powering and adolescent tone to a speech. Slang is, of course, entirely permissible in the relation of a humorous anecdote where it is called for. Similarly on special subjects, such as sport, slang is almost a technical vocabulary and it is bound to be used. But do not use slang for the sake of it; do not use it to show that you are "in" with the crowd.

That is a sort of inverted snobbery and just as much an affectation as the use of unnecessarily long or unfamiliar words. When in doubt, avoid slang.

Vulgarity should always be avoided. It may get a few cheap laughs but the discerning part of the audience will not appreciate it. Avoid the use of swear words, too, even such mild ones as "damned." There are words in the English language which are just as descriptive and which will not cause nearly so much offence. At all costs, and on all occasions, avoid blasphemy.

Be grammatical! Your speech, of course, should be grammatical. There are no special rules about grammar for speeches; in this respect the spoken word does not differ from the written word. You should speak as grammatically as you write, and if you fail on grammar this has nothing to do with speech-making.

Still a few points may be emphasized. Firstly, being grammatical does not mean being pedantic. Grammar was made for man and not man for grammar. Grammar is a good servant and a bad master. Good style in writing as in speaking is certainly essential, but excessive or misplaced regard for grammatical rules may ruin style altogether.

At school you were probably taught that you should never end a sentence with a preposition. It is a sound rule but sometimes it has to be broken. The alternative is to produce an ugly and ungainly sentence. This is bad in writing and worse in speaking. Sir Winston Churchill once ridiculed it brilliantly. He had to read a report prepared by a Civil Servant who had learned the rule too thoroughly and performed all sorts of verbal gymnastics to prevent prepositions from getting to the ends of his sentences. When he had had finished reading the report Churchill wrote in the margin: "This is the sort of English up with which I cannot put."

The famous H. W. Fowler author of several books on the English language had the highest standards, but was broad-minded and tolerant to a degree unusual for a grammarian. He pointed out, for example, that more bad English is written by those who try to avoid splitting infinitives (and yet do not really understand what a split infinitive is) than those who split infinitives carelessly and cheerfully. You often see a needlessly ugly phrase such as "really to be understood," obviously phrased in this ungainly fashion because the writer had the mistaken belief that "to be really understood" contained a split infinitive. Fowler did not recommend splitting infinitives by any means; but he regarded the practice as the lesser evil than distorting sentences to escape from imaginary split infinitives. This is another example of the dangers of trying to be "too grammatical."

Last minute corrections. When you prepare your speech you should always frame it in such a way that you can change it or add to it at the last minute—if necessary in the course of the function at which it is to be made.

This is very important. For one thing, you may be anticipated by a previous speaker saying something—perhaps telling a story—that is already down in your speech. You cannot say the same thing after him, so you must remove it from your speech and, to preserve continuity if not length, close the gap. Another possible reason for having to make a last minute alteration occurs when a previous speaker has said something to which you will be expected to refer or reply. You should not ignore this even if you can do so without making it obvious. Audiences are always favourably impressed when they hear something that the speaker could not possibly have thought out in advance.

A reply to a toast almost always involves last-minute changes and additions. However, such a speech should still be prepared in advance in the normal way, the only difference being that it should be made as general as possible. Usually you can anticipate the sort of things that will be said by the proposer of the toast, and your draft reply should answer these. But you must be ready to change your reply if the things you expect are not said and you must be equally ready to answer points made by the proposer that you have not anticipated.

In this sense replying to a toast is extempore speaking; but that does not mean that the main part of the speech cannot be prepared in advance. In some very formal affairs it is arranged for all the proposers of toasts to let the Chairman have a copy of their speeches. These are then passed on to the various people who are replying to the toasts, so that they know beforehand what points they have to answer.

When you have to make any addition or amendment to your prepared speech the best plan is to make it at the beginning. Usually this is the most suitable place for it. The audience will still have the point fresh in mind and will be expecting you to reply and, moreover, they will be delighted if you reply quickly, apparently without having had much time to think. The main advantage to you is that you can deal with the addition at once, and can then get on with your prepared speech without having to worry about it any more.

Proposing a toast. Many after dinner speeches are in reality toasts, of if they are not toasts in the strictest sense they are quite often incorporated in the speech as such. All the hints given hitherto in this chapter apply to toasts as to other speeches, but a few special factors need to be considered.

One is that the proposer of a toast has the advantage of not having to worry about how to end his speech. He simply invites the audience to drink with him and his closing words are invariably the subject of his toast. This saves a lot of thought, for the ending of a speech is one of the two most difficult parts of it. The other difficult part is, of course, the beginning; and for this, in any social speech and especially in a toast there is rarely anything better than a humorous reference or a humorous anecdote. It saves the speaker from the danger of being banal; it enables him to capture the interest and good humour of the audience at once; and, because it is easy to elate, it gives him confidence in his ability to make the speech.

One more point must be considered in connection with toasts. You have been advised to be sincere in your speeches, and not to say anything that you do not believe yourself. This holds good for toasts, too, although they always call for praise of the person or persons whose health is proposed. If you do not feel that you can sincerely utter such praise, then try as tactfully as possible to decline to propose the toast. If you agree to toast a person whom you can praise with a clear conscience, but of whom you are also critical you must for the sake of courtesy keep the criticism to yourself; but do not exaggerate the praise to make up for it. Exaggerated flattery is bound to be insincere and audiences are quick to detect insincerity. Never put into your speech anything that you cannot honestly say with conviction.

To sum up. When you prepare your speech always bear in mind that your primary object is to make your meaning clear, and the words you use must be chosen primarily for this purpose. The clearest way of saying a thing is usually the simplest. Avoid unnecessarily long words and circumlocutions. Do not say "I obtained a little assistance from the arm of the law" when you mean "I got a lot of help from a policeman." Or, another example, do not say "We came to the parting of the ways" when you mean "We parted."

Never use two words when one will do. Always try for the maximum economy of language. Do not keep saying words like "very" and "quite." Wasting words takes up your time, obscures your meaning, and irritates your audience.

CHAPTER TWO

Delivering the Speech

THE advice given to most would-be speakers—whether it is an After Dinner speech, or some other kind of speech—before they make their maiden effort is to "Stand up; speak up; and shut up!"

In the previous chapter we have already dealt with the need for brevity which covers the last part of this injunction to "Shut up." The rest of the instruction will be covered in this chapter for it is the art of standing up and speaking up which is covered by the one word "Delivery."

Before we can get to the actual point of making the delivery, however, there are still one or two more advance preparations which must be made. Instructions for preparing and writing the speech have already been given; the next step is to memorize the speech.

Memorizing your speech. There are four ways of memorizing a speech. It can be read; it can be learnt by heart and recited; it can be memorized more broadly but not delivered word for word; or it can be so memorized that the speaker will, with the aid of a few notes, be able to deliver it nearly in the form in which it was prepared.

Reading a speech is the very worst method, and it should be avoided. It has many disadvantages. The main one being that it never sounds really convincing, and the audience is unsympathetic from the start. There is the famous case of the speaker who stood up, solemnly produced a sheaf of papers from his pocket, adjusted his glasses and began to read: "It is with considerable surprise that I see so many faces of old friends before me." The old friends laughed—but only because he was reading it and thus giving away the fact that he had written those words before he knew how many old friends would be there. Another disadvantage of reading a speech is that the speaker does not allow himself the opportunity of modifying his speech in the light of what has been said by previous speakers. The necessity for this was mentioned in the previous chapter.

This latter disadvantage applies equally to learning by heart and then reciting. This is not such a bad method as reading, but it is hardly to be recommended. Unless the speaker is naturally a brilliant actor, the speech will probably sound flat and artificial. There is a further danger. Unlike an actor, the speaker has no prompter and, if through an attack of nerves he "loses his place", there will be no one to cue him in and utter confusion and, maybe, panic will result.

The third method is excellent for the practised speaker, but hardly recommended for the beginner. It involves a heavy strain on the memory, and adroitness is the use of words.

The fourth method is probably the most suitable for all but the most accomplished speakers. The work of memorizing the speech is done automatically in the preparation and in the case of a long speech the notes will simply be "abridged notes". That is to say you will make a note of all the main themes in your speech with just sufficient words to remind you of the context of that section of your speech. An example of abridged notes will be found in the chapter dealing with some specimen speeches. You may be dismayed at the thought of not repeating every word of the speech that you took so much trouble to prepare, write and revise; but you can take comfort from the fact that your memory will almost certainly prove an excellent "sieve" retaining the best things and rejecting the worthless.

Where this fourth method of memorizing the speech is used, the notes should be written—or typed, for clarity's sake, on a postcard. They must be clear enough for you to read merely by glancing down. Unless you are short sighted, do not hold the card while delivering the speech, but merely place it on the table in front of you. Consult it with the smallest possible ostentation, preferably during enforced pauses for cheers or laughter. A quick glance down should be enough to assure you of the next point in your speech.

Good delivery can come only with practice and the best practice is to go into a room alone, taking only your card of notes and address an imaginary audience. Having decided not to learn the speech by heart and then recite it, do not keep breaking off while you search your memory for the exact words you wrote. You must be prepared to sacrifice these and you need not think that you were wasting your time in taking so much trouble in composing the speech. Had you not written it out in full and constantly revised it, you would find it much harder to acquire fluency.

That is another reason why this method is preferable to both reading and learning by heart. However hard you may have tried to bear in mind that you were composing a speech and not writing an article, you will almost certainly have included a few sentences that are expressed more in the manner of the written than the spoken word. Your memory censor will come to your help here by rejecting purely "literary" expressions and forcing you to substitute expressions suitable for oratory. This will help greatly to make the speech sound natural.

By making the speech sound natural, we mean that you should try to persuade the audience that it was not prepared beforehand. To this extent the aim of good delivery is to deceive. Firstly you prepared your speech with great care; now in delivering it, you use all your ability to make it sound spontaneous. If the speech were read this would be impossible, and if it were learnt by heart and then recited it would be very difficult.

One of our greatest authors said recently, when making a speech at a distinguished gathering of literary people, that if he had known he would be called upon to make a speech, he would have spent the entire morning working on an impromptu message! And that is the desired result of every speech. However much work and preparation has been spent on it; however much revision pruning, amendment, and curtailing has been done beforehand, the speech itself should always sound as though it has just been made up and delivered "off the cuff".

While you are practising your delivery of the speech with the aid of your notes, you will probably find that in spite of all your careful revision it still contains some things that sound stilted and more suitable expressions will occur to you. Adopt them; do not think that just because your speech has been beautifully written out or typed, therefore it should not be touched. It is never too late to improve and in the matter of speaking, your tongue is always wiser than your pen.

You may find it helpful to try out your speech on a member of your family or a friend. This practice may be useful, but there are some dangers in it. You will almost certainly get some criticism and you must be careful how far you accept such criticism. Consider first if your experimental audience is of the same type as the audience for which your speech has been composed. For example, your wife is not perhaps the best person to judge a speech designed for the Regimental Dinner of your Old Comrades Association. A lot of the humour will be too broad for her taste, and references to past pranks and jokes which will be laughed over in memory by your army friends will probably sound silly to her ears, and she may make you feel that you are taking too juvenile an approach to the matter. It is always easier to amuse a lot of people together than one individual. Even a feeble joke can cause great amusement if there are enough people hearing it together. That is why radio comedians like to have a studio audience.

Control your nerves! Now we come to the actual delivery, the standing up and speaking up. Your first difficulty, at least in your maiden speech, will probably be in controlling your nerves. You will probably be afflicted with what actors call "stage fright". And as any actor worthy of the name will tell you, the performer who does not suffer from "first night nerves" is not a true actor.

Overcoming stage fright is solely a matter of confidence and therefore the first lesson you must learn is that it *can* be overcome. It will help you if you realize that it is a universal affliction of speakers and not peculiar to you. Remember that the most eloquent speakers whom you hear now were probably very nervous and "stage struck" when they first began to speak in public.

There is only one certain way of overcoming nervousness, and that is simply practice. Practice by yourself in an empty room or to the rest of the family—if they will permit it! But whenever you do practice do it properly. Make it a dress rehearsal, as it were, and try to imagine that you are addressing a real audience; otherwise it will be of little help. Practice with the speech you have prepared and also with some of the specimens in this book. To begin with you can simply read these aloud; then try to deliver similar speeches without the book.

When the time comes for you to deliver your speech you will probably find this simple exercise helpful. Just before you are about to rise, deflate your lungs and then take a deep breath, and expel it slowly. Do this two or three times, unobtrusively of course, and you will find it really does help to steady your nerves.

Be careful of seeking "Dutch courage" at the bar or from an extra "stiff" one at the table. A drink may bolster up your confidence temporarily and act as a stimulant; but too much alcohol will certainly be disastrous. It will ruin your delivery and cloud your brain at a time when it should be at its sharpest.

As nerves are felt most at the beginning of a speech, you should have considered this matter in preparing your pre-oration. There is no point in starting with a brilliant sentence if you do not feel you are capable of delivering it properly. A humorous allusion or anecdote is always a good beginning because it is the easiest to relate. Automatically you slip into a natural conversational style and the battle of nerves is won.

Standing up! Everybody who desires to make an impression as an After Dinner speaker must know how to stand properly. But before you stand you have got to rise and the importance of the way you do this is rarely considered. In fact, it is very important indeed.

When you are called upon to get up you probably feel slightly sick, and you want to avoid the gaze of the audience; your legs seem flabby and you may find that you are shaking slightly. Unless you get a grip on yourself you will probably get up slowly and reluctantly and begin with your knees still bent while your feet are shuffling miserably on the floor.

That is no good at all. Get a grip on yourself at once, stand up smartly and face your audience squarely. If you do this you will find that your nerves are much better than they were a few seconds earlier. There is nothing like a show of confidence to make you feel confident.

Your position in standing should be easy and comfortable. The first rule is simple: Don't pose. Don't try to stand like a soldier on parade. Place your feet apart and put yourself at ease.

Don't loll in a slovenly fashion; don't lean heavily on the

table in front of you. Stand upright and don't begin speaking until you have completed the process of standing up. A momentary pause should be made before the speech is begun. It is better to put the weight of your body on one foot rather than on both. For one thing this is less tiring; for another it enables you to turn from one side to the other. But that is not to say that you should be constantly swaying when you are speaking. On the contrary you should keep your body as still as possible. Above all, keep your feet still.

The position of your head is most important. Hold it tilted slightly forward and downward. Don't droop the head so that you look like a wilted daisy, but just hold it easily with the slightest of forward tilts.

Everyone who has ever made any kind of public speech or done any acting at all, knows that the hands are the biggest problem. To the beginner the hands always seem to be enormous and you will just not know how to hold them or what to do with them. There are several ways of easing this problem. First of all don't let them hand limply by your sides, or you will feel and look ill at ease. Don't fold them across your chest or you will not be able to breathe properly. Don't try to rest them on the table in front of you as this will probably be too low and so you will have to bend forward all the time.

Some male speakers like to grasp their coat lapels while they are speaking, but this is only recommended if you can depend upon yourself not to fidget with your hands and twist or roll your lapels round in your fingers. If without a lot of clatter and movement, you can manage to get slightly behind your chair an ideal position is to rest your hands lightly on the back of the chair—provided it is not too low and forces you to bend over. Another very safe place is in your pockets (women speakers often find it easy to slip their hands inside their suit jacket pockets with the thumbs only tucked outside the pocket). If you use pockets, avoid the tendency to fiddle with loose change or keys etc. Finally and this is probably the best since it helps you to stand straight is clasped lightly behind your back.

The position of the hands like everything else is a problem that disappears with practice. The experienced speaker does not think about his hands, and they naturally go into a suitable place.

The matter of gesticulation is simple. First of all never "invent" a gesture. Do not make a deliberate movement of your hands or arms in an attempt to give emphasis to your words. It will make you look like a clown. Therefore do not thing about gestures at all until they come of their own accord. The golden rule about gestures is that they should only be used to illustrate a remark; they should never be meaningless. Above all avoid the laundry mangle action—that is the tendency to move one arm round and round from the diaphragm as you speak. Illustrations of mangle action can be seen all too often on television and films when speakers insist on waving their hands and arms about in this meaningless fashion and it quite definitely distracts from the speech. You will find, as you warm to your subject that you may start making spontaneous gestures. These are natural so do not attempt to alter them. Let them come. The only time you need interfere is when they are coming too frequently. Remember that the British as a nation do not like a lot of demonstrativeness, and if you find that your hands and arms are moving about too much you must control them.

Finally, consider your eyes. Do not look at the ceiling; do not look at the floor. Look at the audience—at the back of the audience for preference. A good tip is to look at one particular member of the audience and speak as if you were speaking to him alone. Only, change your listener from time to time. The unwavering stare of the speaker for more than a minute or so at a time will probably reduce the strongest person to a feeling of mild hysteria. If you are speaking from notes, learn to take them in with an occasional quick glance downward, preferably during a pause.

All these details of posture can be practised beforehand and although they may sound complex at first reading, you will find that they very quickly become automatic and that you fall into the habit of "standing up" correctly almost without thinking.

Don't forget to breathe! Speaking, like singing, requires correct breathing. The first rule is simply that you should stand straight and take as much air into your lungs as you can, and never exhaust them completely. Keeping your shoulders back and your abdomen drawn in slightly will help you to do this. Breathe in more air at every opportunity. Inhale only through the nose if you can; it is important that the taking of a breath should be accomplished in silence. If you are speaking into a microphone this is essential.

Give yourself plenty of opportunity for taking fresh breaths. Do not attempt to deliver too many words without a pause or you will find that you are forced to make an unintended pause simply to take in more air. This can spoil the effect of your speech.

The new or nervous speaker is often detected by the "breathy" way in which he or she talks. The new speaker tends to gasp slightly with each word uttered and it has a very poor effect. Do try not to fall into this error.

Speaking up! It goes almost without saying that a speech should be audible, yet inaudibility is one of the commonest errors in public speaking to-day. Once you have got control of the audience's attention, you will find that the room is quite quiet and that you are able to continue speaking without any conscious effort of having to shout above the noise. But on rising to your feet however, your ears will probably be assailed by the noise of chairs being slightly pulled around for better comfort and vision; of glasses being raised or lowered with a clink; of coffee cups being returned to the saucer with a clatter and you must commence your delivery firmly and clearly enough to overcome all this extraneous noise.

Audibility is quite simple even for those who have not got naturally powerful voices. Anyone can speak clearly and well. First of all open your mouth properly. Don't mutter through clenched teeth or compressed lips. Speak each word clearly, giving full measure to the end of the word. Don't allow yourself to slur or run one word into another. If you want to say "For instance" say each word separately and not just "Fr'instance". When one word ends with an "r" and is followed by a word beginning with a vowel, as in the case quoted above, make quite sure that you don't run the one word in to the other. "Fr'ever" instead of "For ever" is a very common mistake in this direction.

Aim at the back of your audience. There is no need to shout to make your voice carry; clear diction will do all that is necessary. Do not speak too quickly. If you are interrupted by applause or laughter, wait until silence has returned before going on. The same applies to other interruptions. If some of the diners are ill-mannered enough to whisper while you are speaking, do not glare at them; simply pause and they will soon stop their whispering. The same applies if there is any noise made with plate or glass.

During practice you will have divided your speech up into phrases with pauses between them. You will have found from experience that punctuation in speaking is not the same as in writing. You have to make many additional pauses where there are no commas. These pauses should be made intelligently however. A good pause can be more effective than words. Also pauses should be of different lengths. Generally speaking, the more important the words that follow the pause the longer the pause should be. Take these pauses seriously because they are a vital part of your speech. Consider this phrase: "The hospital as you know is badly in need of funds to complete the building of the new wing, and Ladies and Gentlemen this is where we need your

C

help." Read this coolly and unemotionally and the impact
is not very great. Now try speaking this phrase with the
correct pauses allowed for—"The hospital as you know is
badly in need of funds to complete the building of the new
wing,"—PAUSE—"and Ladies and Gentlemen,"—
LONGER PAUSE—(with emphasis) "*This* is where we
need your help." The impact is made, and the audience
have grasped the essential point—that their financial aid is
required. Fit your breathing to the pauses, and not the
pauses to your breathing.

Here is yet another example of the correct use of pauses.
It is that famous tribute made by the outstanding master of
oratory, Sir Winston Churchill, when as war-time Prime
Minister he paid this tribute to the Few during the Battle
of Britain:—

"Never in the field of human conflict was so much owed
by so many to so few."

A clever enough phrase with a neat twist, but consider it
in the way that Sir Winston (then Mr. Churchill)
delivered it:

"Never—PAUSE—in the field of human conflict—
SHORT PAUSE—was so much—SHORT PAUSE—owed
by so many—LONGER PAUSE—to so few." Those of us
old enough to remember the original delivery of the speech
will remember the impact of this phrase. The younger
generation who will have doubtless heard recordings will
appreciate the punch-line power of the sentence.

Not all these pauses are necessary for breathing but they
are all needed to give the words the full significance that
they deserve. It will be seen that the longest pause (of
course, it is only long by comparison) comes before the most
important words "to so few".

Closely linked with the subject of pauses is the use of
emphasis. Again there is a big difference between the
written and the spoken word. When a writer wants to
emphasize a word or phrase he puts it in *italics*. Good

writers use italics sparingly. In speaking, however, "verbal italics" are necessary on a much bigger scale.

For example take the phrase—"It can be done and it will be done." In writing this no italics are needed; but if it is spoken, the verbs must be emphasized so that it becomes: "It *can* be done;—PAUSE—it *will* be done." Emphasis like the pause should be varied. Do not over-emphasize everything or your emphasis will lose its value and you will have nothing left for really important words. Your emphasis should range from light to heavy and be used with care.

Manner of speaking! Your manner of speech will depend upon the occasion and the audience. However certain general principles apply to all circumstances.

Do not be pompous or patronizing; do not "talk down" to your audience; strive rather to win them over to your side. On the other hand do not be over familiar, or you may appear vulgar.

Vary your tone according to the subject matter of your speech. Avoid monotony of delivery. Modulate your tones. Be sincere. Put all the meaning you can into your words, but do not be theatrical. Whatever else your manner is, it must be natural. It should be a polished version of your normal conversational manner. Even if the members of the audience do not know you very well they will be quick to sense artificiality of manner and the receiption of your speech will suffer accordingly.

Do not punctuate your speech with "ums" and "ahs" and "ers." You may not realize it yourself but they are very irritating to the listeners. Watch for this danger from the very start for it can become a habit that is increasingly difficult to cure. The chief cause of this fault is insufficient preparation of the speech. The other main cause is lack of concentration. The speaker say "um", "ah" or "er" to gain time while he thinks of what he is going to say next. If you must pause to think, then let it be a silent pause.

Be articulate. It was said earlier in this chapter that you do not need to have a powerful voice to make yourself audible and it is not volume that makes it possible for your audience to hear what you are saying. It is rather the way you say it.

Speaking is a manner of communication and correct speaking is nothing more than clear speaking. Much snobbishness has been said and written about the question of accent and this can be disposed of very briefly. If you have a Scottish, North country, West country or any other kind of accent, do not try to conceal it. It is nothing to be ashamed of, indeed it gives character to your delivery. The only thing you have to watch is that it should not prevent your audience from understanding what you are saying. Beware of local expressions which mean something else in other parts of the country. For instance, in the North when a person is "starved" it means that they are cold and wet; in the South it means that they are exceedingly hungry.

Use your natural accent. Do not try to adopt for example an "Oxford" accent in the mistaken belief that it is more refined. This will be an affectation and you will neither convince nor please your audience.

Whatever your accent—however you pronounce words— you must make sure that you pronounce them clearly and distinctly. The commonest error in elocution is failure to pronounce certain letters.

Slackness over the letter "h" is well known. Dropping the initial "h" in its commonest form as in words like "house" "horror", "holiday", and "happy". The reverse of the error is to put an "h" in where it does not belong—"H'ambition", "h'always" and so on. A few words beginning with the letter "h" do not need the aspirate sounded in speech. Such words as "heir", "honour", "honest", "hour" do not have the "h" sounded. Some people also drop the "h" from "herb" and "hotel", but this is controversial.

Watch the pronunciation of the word "the". When this comes before a vowel or an "h" mute it should be pronounced "thee"; when before a consonant it is pronounced simply "th" with a short vowel sound to separate it from the first letter of the following word. If this rule is observed it becomes physically impossible to go wrong.

Another common fault is ignoring the "h" in words like "which", "where" and "when". Also watch for slurring in such phrases as "is he"—not "izzee".

The first rule in elocution is that each word should be pronounced separately that all letters that are meant to be pronounced should be pronounced. This may involve making a brief pause between words, but the gain in clearness and distinctness is immeasurable. Letters that often get lost are final "d's" and "t's", and "k's" and the "g" in words ending in "ing". To say "that time" or "and did" correctly involves a definite pause between words. In practising this you may find at first that it sounds stilted and awkward; but with further practice you will eventually find it just as easy to pronounce the words correctly as incorrectly.

The pronunciation of the final "r" depends upon whether or not a vowel begins the next word. In the expression "weather bulletin" for example, the "r" at the end of "weather" is barely pronounced, but if you say "tar and feather" you must pronounce the "r" in tar distinctly. You must not, as has already been said, put in an "r" to join a word ending with a vowel to a word beginning with a vowel as in "the idea of" (*not* "the idearof").

All these errors can be avoided if you practise saying each word slowly and distinctly and pronouncing every letter that is not mute. It is a good plan to practise speaking before a looking-glass to make sure you are using your lips, teeth and tongue in the proper way. Bad vowel sounds are usually the result of failure to open the mouth properly; slackness over the letters "t" and "d" is caused by failure to bring the tongue in proper relation to the teeth.

Most dictionaries give pronunciation as well as definitions, and whenever you are in doubt you should check these.

A common error is putting the wrong stress on a word and you will find that usually the mistake is in putting the stress on the second syllable when it ought to be on the first. Some examples are "ca*pit*alist" for "*cap*italist"; "ap*plic*able" for "*app*licable"; "com*par*able" for "*comp*arable" and so on.

Other errors in pronunciation are the simple result of errors in spelling, usually accompanied by a misunderstanding of the word. Your dictionary will tell you for example the difference between "complacent" and "complaisant"; "effect" and "affect"; "perspicacity" and "perspicuity"; "ingenuous" and "ingenious" and many others.

It will be noted that most of the errors are made in long or relatively long words. This is yet another argument in favour of using short and simple words. Why say "mendacity" when you mean "lying", or "mendicity" when you are referring to "begging". The use of the simpler term would save you a lot of trouble and be much more understandable to your audience.

Final advice. The beginner having read this chapter may now feel a little bewildered with all the many instructions on the correct way to deliver a speech, but constant practise will soon overcome this. Car drivers may remember their very first lesson in driving. One feels that there is so much to do, so many motions to go through that one despairs of ever actually getting the car mobile, but by the time of the third or fourth lesson, most of these actions have become automatic, and by the time we have taken our Test, we scarcely have to think about them—the actions are almost as spontaneous as the action of walking. The same thing applies to delivering a speech; after a few practise runs in front of the bedroom mirror all these things will operate in a perfectly automatic normal fashion and you will be scarcely conscious of performing them. To sum the whole thing up, however, we cannot do better than quote the immortal words of the William Shakespeare in his advice to the players. Through the mouth of his character Hamlet, he says:—

"Speak the speech, I pray you, as I pronounced it to you, trippingly on the tongue; but if you mouth it, as many of your players do, I had as lief the town crier spoke my lines. Nor do not saw the air too much with your hand, thus; but use all gently; for in the very torrent, tempest and as I may say, the whirlwind of passion, you must acquire and beget a temperance that may give it smoothness. Be not too tame neither, but let your own discretion be your tutor; suit the action to the word, the word to the action; with this special observance, that you o'erstep not the modesty of nature."

CHAPTER THREE

Duties of Chairman, President or Host

THE proceedings at a public Dinner or Banquet are usually controlled by a professional M.C. with the co-operation of the Chairman. The Chairman can be in fact the Chairman of the Society, Club or Association which is holding the Dinner; he may be their President, or he may be some local dignitary who is in some way connected with the body who are organising the Dinner. Where there is a professional Master of Ceremonies or Toastmaster, he will make all the necessary announcements, calling upon the various speakers and performing the duties of his profession. However, when the services of a M.C. or Toastmaster are not employed it is the duty of the Chairman to make all the announcements.

The chairman (or host, or president) may make his first announcement when he calls upon any clergyman present to say Grace before the start of the meal. Otherwise his first duty will be to propose the toast of the Queen. This does not call for a speech, he will merely say "Ladies and Gentlemen —the Queen." Following this he will immediately announce "Ladies and Gentlemen, you may smoke." If there are any persons of title present he will, of course, include them in his opening—"My Lord Archbishop, my Lords, Ladies and Gentlemen"; "Your Grace, my Lords, Ladies and Gentlemen"; "Your Royal Highness, Your Grace,

Your Worship, my Lords, Ladies and Gentlemen" and so on according to the circumstances.

Certain of the toasts may be proposed by the Chairman himself and his speech in proposing such toasts is made in the same way as similar speeches by others.

Otherwise the chairman has only to call upon the other speakers whose names and toasts will have been decided in advance. No speech of introduction is needed here. The chairman has only to say "I now call upon Mr. ——— to propose the toast of ———" and "I will now ask Mr.——— to reply to the toast of ——— on behalf of ———."

When there is a musical or other entertainment, the Chairman introduces each item in turn.

At some Dinners it is the practice for the Chairman to call upon various members present to "take wine" with him. This is just a form of exchanging salutations by the means of lifting wine glasses with special guests who may be present. In these cases the Chairman will say "My wife and I will take wine with . . .", and he will then rise to his feet, raise his glass to the guest in question, sip a drink and sit down again. The guest responds in a like fashion at the same time. This practice is not one which is recommended, however, as it means a constant bobbing up and down by the Chairman and the guests so called upon (any ladies involved remain seated; only the men rise slightly to their feet), and it causes a lot of interruptions to the meal. It is far better to finish the business of eating, and then when everybody has relaxed and is sitting back with coffee, liqueurs, cigarettes, cigars, etc., to have all the Toasts and Speeches at one go.

CHAPTER FOUR

Loyal and Patriotic Toasts

1. THE QUEEN.

THIS toast is almost always proposed by the chairman or host. It always heads the toast list; and as smoking is not permitted until this toast has been given the chairman is expected to propose it as soon as possible after the last course of the meal has been finished.

The proposer is not required to make a speech. He simply rises to his feet and utters the time-honoured formula:

"Ladies and Gentlemen—the Queen!"

Immediately after this toast the Chairman should announce:

"Ladies and Gentlemen, you may smoke."

2. THE ROYAL FAMILY.

This toast is much less commonly proposed. Again no speech is required, but the proposer usually gives the toast in the following form:

"Ladies and Gentlemen—I have the honour to propose the toast of the ——— and other members of the Royal Family."

The exact wording of this toast naturally depends upon Royal Births, Marriages and Deaths. However, there is no prescribed formula according to rank and when the toast is to be given the chairman should ascertain the current correct form beforehand. This is issued officially from Buckingham Palace with the approval of the Queen, changes being notified as they occur.

The toasts of the Queen and the Royal Family are the only two loyal toasts that are authorized.

3. HER MAJESTY'S FORCES.

Obviously there must be a patriotic ring about this speech but it should not be overdone and there must not be any suspicion of bombast. The proper note to strike is quiet, sober sincerity, without any striving after effect. If the proposer himself has served in the Forces, a little gentle humour may be introduced as relief, but it must not be pompous or patronizing. If the proposer has never served in the Forces, humour is best avoided, and gratitude and respect should be expressed.

Specimen Speech

Ladies and Gentlemen—I do not think that any sailor, soldier or airman is going to take me to task when I say that we are a peace loving nation. Fighting is not one of our national sports or pastimes. Our only conception of war is self-defence.

It is often said that it takes two to make a quarrel. I suppose there is some truth in this. A quarrelsome person has to find someone to quarrel with, and his victim is not bound to defend himself. In this sense we must plead guilty to having taken part in some long and hard struggles in modern times. But it is worth remembering that if we had not been in this extreme sense such a quarrelsome nation, we should not be a nation at all today. We have a clean record. We have done all possible to avert war and we have taken up arms only when our national existence and freedom have been threatened.

For a people who are so slow and reluctant to fight we have fought pretty well. I say "we" for modern war is total war in which everyone is involved. But although the character of war has changed, let us not forget that the grim business of fighting is still done by the Armed forces. I do not mean to belittle the Home Front when I say that civilians whatever their own efforts, are in the eternal debt of the men who have fought with the enemy on land, at sea and in the air.

Nor is this just a wartime debt. Our Forces not only win wars; they prevent them. Whatever contributions our statesmen and diplomats have made to world peace—and I think they have made many—they would have been powerless without the backing of our Armed Forces.

Our Forces are not numerically large and they have won wars against heavy odds. Their great strength, I think, lies mainly in their efficiency and especially in their high morale. Sane discipline is tempered with individual self-discipline, and it is this latter quality that has made our Servicemen our finest Ambassadors in every part of the world to which duty has taken them.

The toast is to Her Majesty's Forces, and I do not want to discriminate among the different Services that together protect our nation and freedom. Our debt is the same to them all—and to them as a whole, not in parts. Yet I must mention our especial debt to those members of the Services who are professionals. Our regulars not only lead and train our citizen Servicemen; they set the standard of the Services.

Ladies and Gentlemen (or Gentlemen) I give you the toast of Her Majesty's forces and I have pleasure in coupling with it the name of our distinguished guest ————.

4. REPLY TO THE TOAST OF HER MAJESTY'S FORCES.

The reply will be made by a serving member of one of the Forces. Whatever Service he belongs to, he should stress the basic unity of the three Forces and should also pay tribute to auxiliary Services.

Specimen

Mr. Chairman, Ladies and Gentlemen (or Gentlemen)—
The task of replying to this most generous toast fills me with
both pride and alarm. Of the two, I think the alarm is
stronger. In the Army we try to keep in step, but we do not
speak with one voice. Heaven forbid! But I am now called
upon to speak not only for the entire British Army, but for
the Royal Navy and the Royal Air Force as well. The task
is too heavy; and I must ask you to allow me to speak simply
for myself.

The first thing I want to say is that while I am dismayed
at having to reply to this toast, I warmly support the form
in which it has been proposed. You have honoured the three
Services as one whole, and that, I think, is how they should
be considered. Of course every Service has its own traditions, its own customs, and perhaps even its own language;
but at heart we are pretty well at one.

I do not want to suggest that there is no such thing as
inter-Service rivalry. On the contrary, it is very keen—
and this, I would say, is a good thing. Co-operation and
competition are sometimes regarded as opposites, but in
the Services they stimulate each other. As for Service
rivalry, well believe me, the rivalry between the Army and
the Navy or Air Force is quite tame compared with the
rivalry between two of our crack regiments.

You have very kindly paid tribute to those who have made
one of the Services their career. As a professional, I appreciate this; but I want to ask also for your appreciation
of all the other men—and women—who are serving with
us. There are the Volunteer Reserves and Territorials, who
give up their spare time to make their valuable contribution to the defence of our land. Until very recently and
indeed some of them are still with us in the Services, there
were the National Service youngsters, few of whom wanted
to put on uniform, but nearly all of whom accepted the
necessity and pulled their weight. And there are the Women's

Services. We professionals have been called the hard core, but I prefer to think of us as the warp threads. For there can be no warp without weft and no weft without warp; and when the pattern is woven, all the threads are blended into one fabric.

On behalf of this fabric, which is known as Her Majesty's Forces, I thank you.

5. THE ROYAL NAVY.

Again the keynote is sober patriotism. If the proposer of the toast is serving or has served in one of the other Services, he can brighten up his speech with some inter-Service chaffing; but he should not overdo this, and ought to end on a note of sincere respect. If the proposer is not an ex-Serviceman, he should not try to make jokes at the expense of the Service. Historical allusions can be brought in, but should be used sparingly.

Specimen

Ladies and Gentlemen (or Gentlemen)—I now have the honour to propose the toast of the "Silent Service"—the Royal Navy. It may well be silent for it has no need to boast aloud. Its deeds have always spoken for themselves. From the days of King Alfred's first Navy to the Amethyst incident, it has held the supremacy of the seas.

The task of our Navy has been a heavy one. Not only has it had to guard our long island coastline, but it has had to protect our vital sea routes and keep them open for shipping in all the great oceans of the world. As the senior Service it has a great tradition; but at the same time it has always shown itself strikingly progressive. For many centuries naval warfare meant either ships against ships, or ships against shore batteries. In modern times ships have been attacked by two new weapons of deadly striking power, one from above and one from below. Together they constituted a challenge to the very existence of the Navy and, therefore, a challenge to the safety of our island. Our Navy met this challenge and triumphed over it. In the Second World War it protected our lifelines when we were hardest pressed. It rescued our Army from Dunkirk; it supported the R.A.F. in the Battle of Britain; and it led the way to the liberation of Europe on D-Day.

Its losses were heavy; but without it we could not have won the war. It has continued to move with the times and if new weapons are levelled against it in the future, I am confident that it will find the answer to these as well.

Our ships are the finest in the world. But ships alone do not make a Navy. In the old days we spoke of ships of oak and hearts of oak. Nowadays our ships are of steel; and it is not too much to say that with the staunchness of our sailors has evolved in a like manner with their ships. Nothing but iron courage and nerves of steel could have withstood the naval warfare of the last war.

Our Navy is a force of which we can be more justly proud to-day than ever before. I ask you, Ladies and Gentlemen, to drink to the health of the Royal Navy, and I couple with the toast the name of that great sailor ————.

6. REPLY TO THE TOAST OF THE ROYAL NAVY.

Specimen

Mr. Chairman, Gentlemen—I must apoligise for standing up and breaking one of the naval traditions which has just been warmly praised. I have been reminded that the Service to which I have the honour to belong is famous for its silence; and such a compliment deserves a more appropriate reply than a speech.

Nor, indeed, is there anything I can say, beyond expressing my thanks for the most cordial way in which you have received this toast. I would add only this: service in the British Navy is a great privilege as well as a responsibility. In playing our part in the defence of the country we have always known that we have had the trust and confidence of the people behind us. This means a lot to us; and come what may, I promise you that we shall continue to try to be worthy of this trust. Gentlemen, on behalf of the Royal Navy, I thank you.

7. THE BRITISH ARMY.

See under the Royal Navy for Hints on construction of speech.

Specimen

Gentlemen—Khaki is not a glamorous colour, and glamour is not a word that comes to mind when you think of soldiers. Of the three Services, the Army is probably the least showy and spectacular. But it is certainly not the least necessary or the least deserving of our admiration. Even in this atomic age, warfare is still fundamentally territorial. The Second World War was fought with torpedoes and mines, bombs and rockets and all manner of fiendish weapons used at sea and in the air; but the final victory was won on land by the British and Allied Armies.

We have reason to be proud of our Army although it exists, as it were, in spite of our natural inclinations. We are not a militarily minded nation. We do not glory in regimentation. To the average young Briton, putting on a uniform is at the best an unfortunate necessity. Military service is simply a duty to be performed with a maximum of efficiency and a minimum of fuss.

To foreigners our soldiers must appear deceptively harmless. They do not boast or strut or bully. Nowhere in the world can you find troops more modest and restrained in the hour of victory or more decent in their general behaviour. But put these men in a tight corner—and our Armies have been in many tight corners—and they reveal an ability to fight against superior odds that is unique among the Armies of the world. The British, it has been said, never know when they are beaten; and it is only the refusal of the British Army to admit defeat that has saved this nation many times.

Efficiency and fitness, sane but not harsh discipline, initiative and respect for authority, courage and daring and endurance, these are some of the qualitites of our soldiers. But there is another quality which does not belong to individuals. It is team spirit—a part of the British character and nowhere more characteristic than in the British Army.

Gentlemen, I give you the toast of our Army coupled with the name of ————.

8. REPLY TO THE TOAST OF THE BRITISH ARMY.

Specimen

Mr. Chairman, Gentlemen, I wish to thank you most sincerely for the way you have accepted this toast. As a professional soldier I find it heartening to hear such kind words from one of my employers and I am glad to think that you do not consider that you get such bad value for the considerable amount of money that we cost you. I am glad too that you have not clothed the military machine with any false glamour. I will tell you frankly that we know we are, at best, only a necessary evil. We produce nothing, we consume a lot, and we cost a good deal. We occupy valuable ground, we take up housing accommodation, we have to be clothed and fed, and we offer nothing in return unless the country happens to be in danger of attack.

I have been told, very properly, that we are not a militarist nation and it is worth remembering that peace time conscription was quite a recent idea in this country, dating only from the end of the last war. It was not adopted from choice, but from necessity and any comment on its desirability or otherwise in the conditions then obtaining is superfluous. In spite of all that was said about the National Service Army, I can tell you that they were, for the most part, a fine set of lads and whatever their feelings did their job thoroughly and conscientiously. It is not for me to talk about the effect of military service on them; but whatever else it did, I think the Army at least gave them an idea of comradeship and team spirit that was not entirely lost upon them.

Gentlemen on behalf of the Army, I thank you for your generous welcome to this toast.

9. THE ROYAL AIR FORCE.

Specimen

Gentlemen, Our Nation is steeped in tradition and nowwhere is this more apparent than in the Armed Forces. Both our Navy and Army have long and glorious histories. The history of our Air Force is much shorter, but certainly not less glorious. It has shown that tradition does not depend on antiquity, for young as it is, the R.A.F. has already established its own distinctive tradition. (It has even established its own distinctive language too!)

This country has had to fight many critical battles in order to remain free. Some of these have become epics in our history. The Navy had its Trafalgar; the Army had its Waterloo; and the R.A.F. had the Battle of Britain. In each of these battles the enemy fought with superior strength; in each it seemed that only a miracle could save us.

The Battle of Britain was fought and won by young men and when we think of the R.A.F. we think almost instinctively of youth—of youthful energy and daring and amazing courage. The R.A.F. is older now, but the spirit of service seems unchanged.

While we hope and pray for peace, we must preserve our defences; and I do not think it is any exaggeration to say that a strong Air Force is our best guarantee of peace.

Gentlemen, I give you the toast of the Royal Air Force, coupled with the name of ————.

10. REPLY TO THE TOAST OF THE ROYAL AIR FORCE.

Mr. Chairman, Gentlemen, I feel quite unworthy of the honour of replying to this toast. My only qualification is my youth.

I am not going to pretend that I am not proud of belonging to the R.A.F. You, sir, have spoken of it as a young Service, and compared with the Army and the Navy I know it is. But to me it has an almost venerable history which will take a lot of living up to.

I know that we have the reputation of being a bit harebrained, but I want to assure you that we take our flying seriously. Perhaps that is why we run a bit wild when we come down to earth! And I want to add one thing more. Most people when they think of the R.A.F. think only of the aircrew. I ask you to spare a thought for those who keep us in the air—the ground staff who look after the aircraft and make flying safe. Their work is hard and monotonous and all too often it goes unappreciated—by the public at least. But it is appreciated by the aircrew. Our lives depend on the efficiency of the ground staff, and we live to be grateful to them.

On behalf of the Royal Air Force, gentlemen, I thank you for the welcome you have given to this toast.

11. THE REGIMENT.

Specimen

Gentlemen, in these days of centralization, a county does not mean as much as it once did. I am not going to discuss whether this is a good or bad thing; but I must say that I think it would be a very bad thing if county divisions disappeared altogether. Fortunately we can be sure this will never happen. The M.C.C. would never allow it!

Nor I think would the War Office allow such a thing to happen without putting up a strong resistance. And, gentlemen, as you know there are no more stubborn defenders of last ditches than the Whitehall warriors! And they are shrewd as well as stubborn and they know the value of local patriotism. When a man joins the Army he becomes a number, but his Regiment has a name. Our Regiment has not only a name, but a most honourable history. You know of its famous exploits of the distant past, and many of you have participated in its more recent deeds; and I know that nobody here will challenge me when I say that its record will stand comparison with that of any other Regiment in the Army.

If you read the history of our Regiment—and it is a wonderful story—you will find a certain continuity in it. The Regiment has served in many different parts of the world; it has fought many kinds of actions; it has fought with various sorts of weapons and, of course, it has had several generations of soldiers. Yet in every action it has acquitted itself with the same qualities of courage and dash, grit and determination. I am not suggesting that these qualitites are given at birth to everyone who is lucky enough to join our Regiment, but I do say that they are traditional in the Regiment and they are the first things that every new recruit learns to appreciate.

I know you all share my hope that our Regiment will not have to fight another action. It can afford to rest on its laurels, and it is our hope that it will be allowed to do so. But if ever it has to be tested again—well we know that it will again make its name resound all over the land.

Gentlemen, I give you the toast of the Royal ——— Regiment and I couple with it the name of Colonel ———.

12. Reply to the Toast of the Regiment.

Specimen

Gentlemen, I am proud to be able to reply to the toast of the Regiment that I have the honour to command. It is an honour gentlemen, and I am always conscious of it. Our Regiment has had such able and distinguished commanding

officers in the past—I need only to mention Colonel ———
and Colonel ————, that I can hardly hope to live up to
the standard they have set. Fortunately, however, our
Regiment does not depend on its C.O. I might almost say
that it commands itself; for while we pride ourselves on
discipline, we have yet more reason to be proud of the
magnificent self-discipline shown by all ranks. It is my firm
belief that we have the finest officers, the finest N.C.O.'s
and the finest men in the whole British Army. With such a
composition, gentlemen, a Regiment can triumph over
everything, including an indifferent C.O.

I have been told and I know for a fact that the County is
proud of its Regiment, and I assure you that the Regiment
is very proud of the county. It not only gives us our name;
it binds us together. It means that if we are again called
upon to fight to defend England, we shall be fighting
together to defend the same part of England which we all
hold so dear.

On behalf of the ————, gentlemen, thank you.

13. Our Noble Selves.

This toast, which is used at a reunion of some particular
Regiment, Battery, Squadron or Unit where no outsiders
are present. It is generally proposed by the Chairman. While
the speech must have a ring of sincerity it can be pleasantly
informal and the speaker should try to evoke happy
memories of old comradeship.

Specimen

Gentlemen, it is my great privilege to propose the toast of
the finest unit in the British Army. Of course I do not need
to say which unit I am speaking of. I know it was the finest
unit when I served in it and I know it was the finest unit
before I served in it. And I am sure that many of my old
comrades will be quick to tell me that it cannot help but be
even finer now that I am out of it.

Old soldiers, I know, are expected to fade away. I am happy to say that I see no sign of any fading here tonight. On the contrary, unless my memory fails me, it seems to me that most of the old soldiers whom I knew when they were younger are now looming larger than ever.

Not all of us here tonight served in the ———th at the same time. Not all of us have the same memories. No doubt some of the most stirring deeds that took place in my time have failed to be passed down to the next generation. It is even possible that the present members of the unit have never heard of (here insert a reference to a humorous incident connected with someone present at the function), or of (insert another similar reference). If these things have been forgotten, then I feel I am at least serving some purpose in recalling them.

Gentlemen, I am not going to bang a drum in praise of the ———th. It does not need it. We have never advertised our glories to outsiders and we do not have to advertise them to ourselves. We have a great history, and I am sure that we have a great future. Before I close, I must ask you to think of our proudest but saddest possession; our roll of honour. It includes names that are familiar to most of us, men whom we should have liked to have had here tonight. Let us pay homage to them, above all, as we drink—to the ———th.

14. THE WOMEN'S SERVICES

(Usually proposed by a member of H.M. Forces).

This is a general toast like the toast to Her Majesty's Forces; toasts to the particular branches of the Women's Services will follow much the same lines as those given for the men's services, with suitable alterations to fit the circumstances. These toasts are most generally given by men who are or who have been serving members of the armed forces. The keynote of each speech should be appreciation of the work women do, and the speaker must be careful to avoid any hint of patronage or condescension.

Specimen

Mr. Chairman, Ladies and Gentlemen, Serving one's country, like voting, used to be a man's job alone. The women's job was to keep the home fires burning; and if it had been left to the men, that is all they would still be doing. For no one can say that the men dragged them out of their homes any more than it could be said that women were dragged to the polls. The Women's Services came into being as a result of the demand of the women themselves. That demand was conceded rather grudgingly and with many head shakings by men who were convinced in advance that women would never make soldiers.

I do not need to remind you of the way in which the Women's Services have proved themselves. They served with great distinction in two world wars, and their heroic work in the Mixed Batteries and in other fields is now a part of military history.

Many Servicemen were inclined at first to think of their probable value as mainly ornamental. Please don't misunderstand me, I should be the last person to underrate their decorative qualities. But we soon found that they had not come merely to brighten up the lives of the troops. They were in uniform to do a job of work and the way they did their job won the admiration of us all. After the First World War the Women's Services were stood down. They returned for the Second World War and made themselves so indispensable that they now have permitted peacetime establishments. They have won their colours the hard way and now the men of the Forces are proud to acknowledge them as their comrades in uniform.

Ladies and gentlemen, I ask you to join me in this salute to the gallant women—I should prefer to call them ladies but they would not allow it—of the Services.

15. REPLY TO THE TOAST OF THE WOMEN'S SERVICES.

Specimen

Mr. Chairman, Ladies and Gentlemen. Thank you for the kind way in which you have received this toast. I would almost suspect you of flattery and being a woman, I should not seriously object to that, were it not for the fact that in my Service life I have had so many proofs of the goodwill of the men's Services. It is true, I agree that we had to demand to be allowed to share in the defence of our country, but I do not think that the early objections were based entirely on the grounds that have been suggested. Rather it was man's natural instinct of chivalry that wanted to spare us from possible hardship and danger.

It is not surprising that we get on so well with the men's Services. As you know, there is something about a soldier; all the nice girls love a sailor; while those R.A.F. types are simply irresistible. Co-operation with the men's Services has often been so close that it has ended at the altar. Did I say ended? That was the last thing I meant!

I must say how much we appreciate the way in which the men take us seriously, trust us to do our job and let us get on with it. Please do not think that we imagine that our contribution is, or can ever be, equal to that of the men who have to go out and fight, but we are proud to do our bit alongside those who protect our land.

On behalf of the Women's Services, I thank you!

16. THE NURSING SERVICES.

Simple admiration should be the keynote of this speech and praise should be sincere rather than extravagant.

Specimen

Ladies and Gentlemen, I have great pleasure in proposing the toast of the Nursing Services. This toast hardly needs a speech for our debt to the Nursing Services is too well known. Nursing the sick is service in its highest form, service involving hard work and bringing little material reward. It demands unselfishness, a will to work and above all, a sense of vocation.

Our nurses are our heroines in peace and war. They receive few decorations. All too often they are taken for granted. While we rightly revere the name of Florence Nightingale, we are all too apt to overlook the fact that the tradition of the "Lady with the Lamp" is still carried on. The name of Edith Cavell conjures up a picture of unique courage and devotion to duty are integral parts of the very spirit of the Nursing Services today.

Our Nurses prefer to carry out their tasks anonymously and they seek no praise. I shall not embarrass them further. Ladies and gentlemen, I ask you to drink to the health of the Nursing Services, and I couple with this toast the name of Sister —————.

17. Reply to the Toast of the Nursing Services.

Specimen

Ladies and Gentlemen, Thank you for the kind welcome you have given to this toast. Really I think it was too kind, for we nurses are very ordinary human beings. I am not going to pretend that nursing is not hard work nor that we don't sometimes find it tedious; but by and large we do it because we like it and that seems a good reason for doing any job. For anyone who didn't like the work I imagine it would be pretty hateful; but for our part we count ourselves lucky to be doing something that appeals to us.

And I must add a word about our patients. I expect that most of you will have been in our hands at some time or other, so I can make it quite personal when I say that for the most part we like our patients. There are a few exceptions of course—and in my experience the biggest grumblers are the ones who have the least wrong with them. Many of the more seriously ill cases that I have nursed have shown such appreciation and good humour that it was a positive joy to do what little I could to ease their suffering. For although a doctor, and especially a surgeon, may have to consider the disease more than the patient, for us nurses sickeness is a very human matter and I know of no finer sight in the world than a sick person smiling bravely in spite of suffering. It is that sort of sight that makes nursing really worth while.

On behalf of the Nursing Services, ladies and gentlemen, I thank you.

CHAPTER FIVE

Civic Toasts

18. THE MAYOR AND CORPORATION.

THIS toast is generally proposed at a Civic Dinner where the Mayor is known personally by many of those present. A personal element should therefore be introduced into the speech—for example, if it is known that the Mayor is a keen golfer, some humorous reference should be made of the fact.

Specimen

Ladies and Gentlemen, I am happy to have the duty of proposing the toast of the Mayor and Corporation. Most of us, I am afraid, are in the habit of taking the Corporation for granted. What is worse on the few occasions we do think about it, our thoughts are not always kindly. We remember the Corporation when there are elections—and then, of course, the Corporation remember us; and we remember it especially twice every year when we get the rates demands. Otherwise we seem to forget that the Corporation exists. My only defence for this apparently ungrateful attitude is that it shows, far better than any words could do, just how efficiently the Corporation does its work. It never lets us down.

But although we may take the Corporation for granted, the same does not apply to the Mayor. He is not the sort of man you can ignore. He is a personality—a character. He leaves his mark on everything he does. If you do not believe me, I invite you to go up to the golf course and have a look at the bunker behind the green at the fifteenth hole. There you will see what a worshipful niblick did three months ago.

However I am not being fair. Our Mayor, as you know, is tireless in the performance of his many public duties and we have every reason to be grateful to him. Both he and all the members of the Corporation labour unstintingly for the good of the community. They set a magnificent example in local government—and I only wish that the Governments of the world were in similar hands.

Ladies and gentlemen, I ask you to drink to the health of our Mayor and Corporation.

19. REPLY TO THE TOAST OF THE MAYOR AND CORPORATION.
Mr. Chairman, Ladies and gentlemen—You are very kind—much kinder than we deserve. We of the Corporation are not particularly modest folk, but I am sure my colleagues will want me to say that we have not earned all your compliments. For the fact is that we do comparatively little. The real work is done by the various officers who put local government into effect. I know that the standard of local government in this country is exceptionally high, but I am convinced that it is nowhere higher than it is here. Why, they even manage to collect the rates!

Still, I fear I am doing an injustice to my colleagues. They do work and they work really hard. The only person at the Town Hall who is idle is myself. This may surprise you, I hope it does for I have always tried to look busy, but it will not surprise you more than it did me when I assumed office. I will tell you frankly that I had been dreading the day, wondering how on earth I could carry out all the numerous duties that would be expected of me. Groundless fears; the duties were there all right, but the work was done for me.

Therefore, ladies and gentlemen, it is with some pangs of conscience on my own behalf, but not on the behalf of my colleagues, that I thank you most sincerely for the cordial reception you have given to this toast.

20. HER MAJESTY'S JUDGES.

The task of proposing this toast is usually given to an experienced speaker. The speech needs to be good with some real wit, because the reply will almost certainly be an example of good oratory. Humour is essential here.

Specimen

Ladies and gentlemen, the task of proposing this toast fills me with alarm. This is not because I am frightened of Her Majesty's Judges in general and certainly not through any particular fear of Mr. Justice ――, whom we are so happy to see here tonight. For by a fortunate chance Mr. Justice ―― is one of Her Majesty's Judges who has never had to pass judgment on me. I do not fear him for his power—yet I fear him for another reason. He will reply to this toast; You may be sure you will hear a speech of great wit and eloquence, which will make my present effort seem even feebler than it is.

There is a common belief in this country that Judges are rather dry, inhuman men who live part in a world of torts and malfeasances, and really have little idea of everyday life as the rest of us know it. Many Judges, of course, deliberately foster this idea. For hours they sit in silence apparently unmoved by either the eloquence of the barristers or the pathos and drama of the evidence of witnesses. You wonder if they are really alive. Then when you have almost given up hope, the Judge leans forward and with a slightly puzzled frown, asks some such question as: "Who is Miss Marilyn Monroe?"

This almost unbelievable ignorance, and I am stretching a point when I say it is only *almost* unbelievable, contrasts strangely with the omniscience of the barristers. They know everything about everything. One day a barrister is speaking with all the authority of an economist; the next day he is arguing equally impressively on the proper way to prune roses.

Now as Judges would have us believe that they know nothing about economics or pruning roses, one may wonder what they were doing before they were elevated to their high office. From when came they? The answer, as you know, is that they came from the Bar. Please do not misunderstand me. The Bar I am speaking of is a very dry one—dry as dust in fact—with so much dust that the barristers even find enough to try to throw into the eyes of the jury. So that a Judge who now professes ignorance even of the existence of Miss Marilyn Monroe was himself once an expert on economics, horticulture, and every other subject that comes the way of a barrister.

The explanation for this change is not so difficult to find. A Barrister and a Judge have only one thing in common; knowledge of the law. In at least one vitally important respect they are utterly.different. The Barrister prosecutes or pleads. He is frankly partisan. The Judge is impartial. That, I think, is why a Judge becomes a different person from the man who used to be a Barrister.

Be that as it may, I am sure you will all agree with me, when I say that Her Majesty's Judges enjoy not only our respect and admiration, but our confidence. There is no rough justice in this country and no innocent man needs to fear wrongful conviction.

Ladies and gentlemen, I have great pleasure in asking you to drink the health of Her Majesty's Judges, and I couple with this toast the name of Mr. Justice ——.

21. THE MAGISTRATES.

This speech does not call for the same standard of oratory as the toast of Her Majesty's Judges, and a more personal element may be introduced if the magistrates present are well known to the speaker and his audience.

Specimen

Ladies and gentlemen, I have a vague recollection from my schooldays that when I had finished the dozen different ways of expressing the Latin for a table. I was put on to declining a noun called "magister". I believe that it is from this word that "magistrate" comes; and I know that it means "master".

This seems very appropriate, for in the presence of a magistrate I feel very much like a schoolboy in the presence of his master. Indeed if I remember rightly we used to refer to our Head as "the beak".

By quite extraordinary and sustained good fortune, I have not yet been brought before our magistrates. I expect this will surprise you; it is a constant source of amazement to me. But when my day does come—as I fear it must—I invite you all to come to court and hear what the clerk says when he is asked if I am "known".

Perhaps because of my lack of knowledge of the magistrates in their official capacity, I am very happy to propose their health. The Bench is held in deservedly high esteem, and I am sure you will agree with me when I say that we are particularly lucky in this respect. Ladies and gentlemen, the magistrates.

22. REPLY TO THE TOAST OF THE MAGISTRATES.

Specimen

Ladies and gentlemen, It is a novel and refreshing experience for me to receive such cordial good wishes for my health in public. More commonly I hear expressions of hope for my early demise. From the cordial reception you have given to this toast I can only conclude that you all have very clear consciences and that none of you expect to appear before the Bench. May I offer you my congratulations and, in return, express my hope that you will all continue to keep clear of the Law.

If, however, you contemplate a life of crime, it would seem that now is an excellent time to start. You are well aware, I am sure, that magistrates are crusty folk and that the severity of their sentences they impose depends mainly on their physical well-being and state of their livers. My criminal friends assure me that it is always better after lunch, provided that the lunch was a good one. All magistrates are bad, of course; but a well-fed magistrate is not so bad as a hungry one. A liverish magistrate is the worst of all.

At the moment I am extremely well fed, and I certainly shouldn't have the heart to send any of my fellow-diners to the galleys. But I must give you a warning. If you decide to crack a crib or park your your car on the wrong side of the road, or commit some equally heinous offence, I urge you to do it as quickly as possible and, if you are caught—as you will be, of course—to insist on an immediate appearance in Court. If you wait till tomorrow morning you will certainly find me suffering from indigestion and very liverish.

So far I have been speaking only on my own behalf. But your toast was to the Bench as a whole, and on behalf of my fellow magistrates I must speak more cautiously. I know they would want me to express my appreciation of your hearty good wishes, because I know that they share my view that those who are privileged to assist in the administration of the Law should try to earn the goodwill of the community that the Law is designed to protect. British justice is something of which we can all be proud, and one of the reasons for our pride is that the magistrates have strictly limited powers. In some countries a magistrate is regarded with fear by the innocent as well as by the guilty. Here, I think I can say, even the guilty have no need to fear that they will get any worse punishment than they deserve.

Ladies and gentlemen, thank you again.

23. THE POLICE FORCE.

Usually this toast is proposed at a local dinner—such as a Municipal Dinner. In such circumstances, the speaker is usually a member of the municipal council who is not connected with Police. The subject offers plenty of scope for humour, but this should not be overdone; nor carried at the expense of a genuine tribute to the work of the Police.

Specimen

Ladies and gentlemen, when American visitors come to this country and are asked for their impressions, many of them—especially the women—begin by saying "I think your policemen are wonderful". For some peculiar reason this is generally regarded as a huge joke. Why it should be I cannot imagine; for I am not an American visitor, nor yet am I a woman, and I have never ceased to think that our policemen are wonderful.

Of course I must admit that I am prejudiced. Although I have lived a long life of crime, I have never been found out. Please don't think that this is because the police aren't up to their job; I am just the exception that proves the rule, and I hope if I go on saying nice things about them they will allow me to remain exceptional.

So far I have had only one brush with the police, and that was not really a brush. It was over a little matter of parking on the wrong day or the wrong side, or probably both. I got off with a fatherly lecture and a promise to be a good boy in future.

Our Police are wonderfully fatherly, not only to the children who want to be helped across the road, but to men and women old enough to be their grandparents. Yet the thing that makes them so really wonderful is their good humour. You never see a bad-tempered policeman. You never find a policeman discourteous or even officious. Watch the way the Police handle a demonstration or a noisy crowd. They maintain order not by threats or blows, but by good humour and common sense. That is their particular genius.

Yet sometimes I wonder if we really appreciate what the Police do for us. I do not mean merely in its positive actions, but in its power to prevent crime. There are many views held these days on the value of punishment as a deterrent, and it is not my place to give a personal opinion on this subject. But I must express my absolute conviction that the greatest deterrent to crime is a strong and efficient Police Force. The criminal's concern about the punishment he will receive if he is caught is a secondary consideration; the thing that worries him most and makes him think twice before committing a crime is what the chances are of his being caught. Our greatest safeguard against crime is not the severity of the Law, but the figure of the policeman on the corner. And let us never forget that the policeman is always there; for whatever the provocation the Police never go on strike.

Ladies and gentlemen, I ask you to drink to the health of the Police Force and I couple with this toast the name of Inspector ——.

24. Reply to the Toast of the Police Force.

Specimen

Ladies and gentlemen, I am happy to reply on behalf of the Police Force to the generous welcome you have given to this toast. Flattering things have been said about us, and I am almost tempted to say that I wouldn't have the heart to arrest the proposer of the toast even if I did catch him out. But you know policemen have no hearts.

I am not going to indulge in false modesty and contradict the compliments that have been paid to the Police Force, because I am proud enough to think that it compares well with the Forces in other countries. But the credit for this is not ours. It is yours. Nowhere in the world is there such a peaceful, law-abiding people as in Britain. A Police Force may be described as the discipline of the Law; and discipline has to be enforced only when self-discipline is absent. In this country self-discipline is a common possession.

You have spoken of the good-humoured way in which the Police deal with noisy crowds and demonstrations. The simple fact is that good humour is the only language a British crowd understands. The crowds themselves are so good-humoured that no other treatment is possible.

Finally I should like to say that we regard ourselves not only as the custodians of the peace but also as the servants of the public. And it is a good public and a good service to be in. Thank you, ladies and gentlemen.

25. THE FIRE BRIGADE.

Specimen

Ladies and gentlemen, I am going to let you into a secret. When I was younger and wiser—and on both counts that means many years ago—I had one great ambition in life. That was when I grew up, I should become a fireman.

Well, I never achieved that ambition. That was my loss— although, no doubt, it is the Fire Service's gain. But I never really succeeded in conquering the desire, and today as in those early years, I am always thrilled and excited when I see a gleaming fire engine racing along the street with the bell clanging and the firemen tense and ready for action.

Fortunately I have never had to entertain the Fire Brigade at home in its official capacity. I have seen it at work else-where, however, and I have marvelled at the skill and courage of the men. And I have been over the scene of a fire after it has been put out by the Brigade, and I have marvelled again at the way in which property has been saved from damage. The Brigade's greatest work is the saving of life, and you know what heroism is shown for this purpose. But the Brigade also saves property, and the men

who fight the fire show such wonderful skill and restraint—
often at great personal danger—that much is preserved
that would surely be lost under less careful hands.

We are lucky in this district. We have a Fire Brigade that
can hardly have any equal in efficiency of organisation and
personal zeal. It is the best insurance policy we have, for it
gives us a feeling of secutiry that could not otherwise be
obtained.

Ladies and gentlemen, I ask you to drink to the men of
our Fire Brigade.

26. REPLY TO THE TOAST OF THE FIRE BRIGADE.

Specimen

Ladies and gentlemen, I am happy to reply to your kind
toast to the Fire Brigade. We do not deserve the compliments you have paid us, for happily it is not very often that
we have to fight a really big fire. You may be interested to
hear a few statistics. In the last month, we have answered
fourteen calls. As a result of this activity we put out two small
fires; observed the remains of two others that were privately
extinguished before our arrival; observed vague evidence
of two more that had not got the strength to keep burning
for us; sought hard for three fires that were reported but
never seem to have caught alight; and rescued five cats
from uncomfortable positions that had nothing to do with
fire at all.

Please do not think I am complaining about the shortage
of fires. On the contrary, I want to thank you all for the care
you show in preventing outbreaks. We should prefer you to
train your cats to study their lines of retreat; but we would
rather rescue your cats than have to break your windows
and ruin your personal possessions with water.

Ladies and gentlemen, on behalf of the Fire Brigade I
thank you.

CHAPTER SIX

Toasts for Church Dinners and School Reunions

27. THE BISHOP.

THIS toast is usually proposed by the chairman (a layman) at a mixed gathering of clergy and laity. The theme should be the hard work put in by the clergy in general and the Bishop in particular. Humour, unless very gentle, is not recommended for any but a practised speaker, and the speaker should be careful to avoid any controversial subject.

Specimen

Ladies and gentlemen, it is my honour and privilege to ask you to drink to the health of our Bishop. It would be impertinent of me to try to tell you of the great work he does in our Diocese and in any case this would be impossible. You all know much of what the Bishop has done for us; but you know, too, that he does very much more which is concealed from public notice. Our Bishop does good with such stealth that he is rarely found out, even by accident. I have caught him out once or twice but I am not going to give him away.

Tomorrow we shall have the pleasure of hearing the Bishop preach. Those who have heard him before know that this will be indeed a pleasure. But it is not merely as a great preacher that our Bishop demands our respect; it is rather by the example that he sets us. He does not only tell us how we can lead the Christian life; by his own life he shows us what a Christian is.

Ladies and gentlemen, I have great pleasure in proposing the health of the Bishop.

28. THE CLERGY.

Specimen

Ladies and gentlemen, I am happy to have the privilege of proposing the health of our Bishop and clergy. Our debt to them is considerable. Not only are they our spiritual advisers and helpers, but they are also our friends. It is impossible to estimate how much good they have caused, and how much evil they have prevented by their social work in our Diocese. They would not like to hear any estimate of this kind, even if it could be made, for individually and collectively they prefer to hide their lights under bushels.

We are very happy to have the Bishop with us to-day. We do not see him very often, but we know that the Diocese is large and others need his presence, as well as ourselves. I must, however, express our appreciation of the magnificent work he has done, which is the inspiration of all who try to lead a Christian life.

Ladies and gentlemen, I give you the toast of the Bishop and his Clergy.

29. THE VICAR.

This speech can be a little less formal and more humorous than one given for the Bishop and Clergy—particularly, if the Vicar is a friend of the speaker.

Specimen

Ladies and gentlemen, Popularity, like happiness, is elusive for those who seek it, and yet comes easily to those who never think about it. That is why our Vicar is such a popular man. I have never known him do or say a single thing for the sake of public favour. I have known him do and say several things that seemed likely to incur public disfavour. Yet the fact is that there is no one in this parish who is so well loved and respected as our Vicar. He is our guide, counsellor and friend—a good companion on sunny days, and a sympathetic and wise adviser and helper when things go wrong.

Our Vicar is certainly not a worldly man, but he is a man of the world. I can think of no department in our parish life in which he does not play an active part. He is a star turn at our concerts. On the cricket field his leg-spinners have gained a reputation that I can only describe as unholy. His presence gives zest to every social function we have. I am told that no Women's Institute function would be worth holding without the Vicar and I know that the ladies regard him as well, gentlemen, there are too many husbands here for me to continue with this theme.

Nothing that I can say can do full justice to the Vicar, so I shall say no more, and just ask you to join me in drinking his health. Ladies and gentlemen—The Vicar.

30. The Churchwardens.

Ladies and gentlemen, the work of the Church, like the game of cricket is shared between amateurs and professionals or Gentlemen and Players. Speaking as one of the least distinguished of the Players a No. 11 batsman if ever there was one—I have the happy task of proposing the health of the Gentlemen and in particular of those fine all-rounders the Churchwardens.

My dictionary gives three definitions of a warden. The first describes him as a watchman or sentinel, but this definition is parenthetically—and it seems to me disparagingly—labelled "archaic". The second definition is that the warden is a guardian, president or governor as of a college. Finally my dictionary tells me, rather surprisingly, that a warden is a kind of cooking pear.

Now, ladies and gentlemen, the second definition is clearly inappropriate. Our Churchwardens are not presidents nor governors, although I have not the slightest doubt that they would make very good ones, nor, I think can they be fairly labelled as cooking pears. They are the wrong shape for that. So we must fall back on the first definition, which seems admirable except for the word "archaic". This is most unfair, for they are both energetic and active.

But they are certainly watchmen and sentinels. As amateurs, or Gentlemen, in the team, they keep us professionals up to scratch. As good all-rounders they take a big share in both the batting and bowling, and it is hard to imagine how we could manage without them.

Ladies and gentlemen, I ask you to give a hearty response to the toast of The Churchwardens.

31. REPLY TO THE TOAST OF THE CHURCHWARDENS.

This speech, made by one of the churchwardens, is largely governed by what was said by the proposer of the toast. Generally speaking, however, it will consist of a modest disavowal of the kind things said by the previous speaker, and an expression of pleasure in the duties of churchwardens. This speech needs humour.

Specimen

Ladies and gentlemen, Our Vicar has said some very kind things about us Churchwardens, and he has put me in a very difficult position. If I accept all these compliments without demur, I shall not only be lacking in modesty, but also guilty of suppressing the truth. If, on the other hand, I deny the justice of his remarks, I shall be suggesting that the Vicar himself has not been speaking the truth. Now you all know that the Vicar is the most honest of men, and that he is quite fearless in the matter of speaking the truth. You must therefore be puzzled to know how he can have come to say such nice things about men who have done nothing to deserve them. Fortunately, there is an answer to the question which both absolves the Vicar from the charge of dishonesty and yet puts us Churchwardens in our proper place.

The fact of the matter is simply that the Vicar has a happy habit of seeing the good in the worst of us. He showed this to me quite clearly the other day, when we made a train journey together. According to the time-table we should have arrived at our destination just in time for lunch; but in fact we still had a fair way to go when lunch-time arrived. I put this down to the inefficiency of the railway, but the Vicar's opinion was that he must have made a mistake in reading the time-table. That, by the way. The train stopped at a station and we learned that it was un-likely to remain there for more than a minute or so. Rather regretfully we decided that there was no time even for a dash to the buffet to get something to eat. However a rather grimy little boy was standing on the platform, and the Vicar beckoned to him.

"Here's a shilling," he said, "Now will you go to the buffet and buy three fourpenny buns, and bring back two for my friend and myself. The other one is for you."

The boy seized the shilling and dashed off to the buffet. I shook my head sadly.

"I don't think we'll see him again," I said, "Or your shilling either."

The Vicar chided me gently for my lack of faith in human nature.

"He'll come back," he said confidently. And I knew it was useless to argue for even if the boy did not come back the Vicar would have found some excuse for him.

As it happened, however, the boy did return with a bun wedged firmly in his mouth. But that was the only bun he had, and when he reached the window of our carriage he thrust eightpence into the Vicar's hands.

"Sorry," he said between mouthfuls. "They only had one left."

And then, gentlemen, the Vicar thanked him gravely and turned to me—

"You see? I told you he was an honest lad."

And that story, I think, explains why you have heard things said about the Churchwardens that must differ greatly from your own knowledge of us. Ladies and gentlemen, on behalf of my colleagues, I thank you.

32. THE SCHOOL REUNION.

Gentlemen (or Ladies, if it is an Old Girls' Dinner), The Old School Tie has been the subject of so many music hall jokes that one might expect it to have been laughed out of existence. Yet there seems to be plenty of evidence to the contrary here tonight; and the fact that it has survived so much ridicule surely proves that it is by no means a meaningless subject.

Most loyalties are difficult to explain, and loyalty to the School is no exception. Old Boys' (Girls') Associations differ from most other societies in one important respect, their members are not proposed and elected, and indeed have little say in the matter of qualification for membership. The only thing that we have in common, on the face of it, is that our respective parents happened to send us to the same educational establishment; and one might ask what bond can exist among us. The answer is not far to seek. As boys we were drawn together in comradeship, not because we liked the look of each other's faces—I am sure you will agree with me on this point—but through loyalty to a common ideal.

The strength of that ideal lies in the fact, of which we have abundant evidence here now, that it continues to hold us together after the end of our communal life. It is not easy to express its source of inspiration. It has nothing to do with the School's scholastic or sporting achievements; it does not derive from the School buildings or grounds; it does not even come from the headmaster and the teaching staff—saving their presence—although without their good influence it could hardly survive. It is simply one of those imponderable, and can only be defined as the Spirit of the School—a spirit compounded of honour, teamwork, comradeship and all that is best in communal life.

Gentlemen (Ladies)—The School.

CHAPTER SEVEN

Social Toasts

33. OUR MEMBER OF PARLIAMENT.
THE toast to the local M.P. may be proposed at a purely
Party gathering or at a function where the audience is
more general. In the latter case the speaker should steer
clear of political controversy, for the proposal of a toast
should be so worded that the toast itself will be readily
accepted by the whole audience.

Specimen

Ladies and gentlemen, It is with great pleasure that I
rise to propose the toast of our Member of Parliament. This
is not a political function and I am not going to make a
political speech. Indeed, I am not going to make any kind
of a speech at all, for I am sure that after the last stormy
session in Westminster, Mr. ——has heard enough speeches
to last him until the end of the recess.

So all I want to say is this. Whatever our Member has
said in the House of Commons—and he may be surprised
to know how closely we read his speeches—he has never
forgotten the interests of his constituents. On several
occasions he has spoken up on our behalf, even at the risk
of making himself unpopular with the Party to which he
belongs; and ever since he was elected, he has, I know,

personally investigated every request and complaint that he has received from a constituent. His presence with us to-day is one more example of his concern with local affairs; and when he next presents himself to the electorate, whether we put him in again or cast him out into the political wilderness, he may rest assured that the efforts he has made on our behalf as a community will have been both recognised and appreciated.

Ladies and gentlemen, I give you the toast of Mr. ——, our M.P.

34. THE LADIES.

This toast is usually proposed by the youngest bachelor at Dinner, and the spirit of the choice should be reflected in his speech. It should be light-hearted but, of course, flattering to the ladies. Humour is naturally desirable but the speaker should exercise particular care to ensure that his jokes are in good taste. If a joke seems only a shade doubtful it is better left out.

Specimen

Gentlemen, the task of proposing this toast has been given to me because I happen to be the youngest bachelor here tonight. I do not know the origin of this custom, but I imagine it must be because the youngest is the least likely to be a confirmed bachelor, and his single state is probably not due to any lack of appreciation of the opposite sex. In my own case I may as well admit that I am full of appreciation. The ladies here tonight have only a poor speaker to extol their charms, but they could not find a more devoted admirer.

I hope you will not think that because I am single, I know nothing about the ladies. I have not, of course, the same concentrated experience of a married man, but no doubt that will come later. Meanwhile I am steadily enlarging my knowledge of the fair sex in general—at least, to the extent that they will allow me. And every enlargement of my knowledge adds further to my admiration. The fact is, gentlemen, that the time seems to be approaching when I shall not be able to keep away from them!

We sometimes hear talk, even in these modern times, of the so-called equality of women as though it were something to be argued about. I am neither a social historian nor a prophet, but I venture to suggest that such a thing as equality between the sexes has never existed and never will exist. Women have never been our equals; they have always been vastly superior to us. There would be more sense in talking about equality for men, but personally I hope it never comes to that. Let the ladies remain as different, as feminine, and as irresistible as they are now.

I ask you to join me in drinking to the health of those wonderful creatures—Gentlemen, The Ladies!

35. Reply to the Toast of the Ladies.

Specimen

Gentlemen, My difficulty in replying to your most generous toast is that I am not allowed to say what I want to. You are allowed to flatter us as much as you like—and almost as much as we like, but the only times when we are allowed to tell you what we think of you are when our thoughts are unfriendly. The primmest Victorian miss always had the right to say to a man, "Sir, your attentions are unwelcome; pray desist"; but today even for all our much vaunted freedom, no girl would dare to say to a man, "Sir, your attentions are very welcome, please carry on." That would be regarded as immodest if not worse. All women are expected to have a natural modesty; but I suspect that the Frenchman Balzac got nearest the truth when he said that "woman's modesty is man's greatest invention."

So here I am, allowed to say no more than thank you for the very kind compliments you have paid us. I dare not tell you in reply that I have been an admirer of men almost from the cradle; that I find you good to look at, pleasant to listen to, delightful to dance with, charming companions; that in fact, I think you are wonderful! These are the things I dare not say—but perhaps now you will be able to guess them.

36. OUR GUESTS.

All the specimen speeches in this book are particular to one set of circumstances and need to be adapted to suit the occasion. This applies most of all to the toast of "Our Guests". There are so many countless occasions when this toast is proposed and each one is different from the others. The main thing, however, is that the proposer should include in his speech some complimentary allusions to the more prominent guests—including, of course, the guest who had been chosen to reply to the toast.

Specimen

Ladies and gentlemen, it is my privilege to propose the health of our guests. It is an easy task and requires few words and no formality from me ; for most of our guests are not strangers. I hope that by the time they leave they will all think of themselves as our friends.

Some of our guests have travelled quite a long way to be with us tonight and I know I am expressing the general opinion when I say how much we appreciate the compliment they have paid us in spending the evening with us. I only hope that they will not regret their kindness. I am reminded that the late George Bernard Shaw was once a guest at a social function and was asked afterwards what the company was like. "Terrible," he replied, "I should have been bored stiff if I hadn't been there." I hope none of our guests will think this worth quoting when they are asked the same question.

We are pleased to have with us tonight (here include

the names and some allusions to the prominent guests).

Finally I want to say how much pleasure the presence of all our guests has given to us, and to express the hope that we shall have many opportunities of seeing more of them in the future and getting to know them better.

Ladies and gentlemen, I give you the toast of Our Guests!

37. REPLY TO THE TOAST OF OUR GUESTS.

Specimen

Ladies and gentlemen, when a man has been wined and dined in this regal fashion, his only concern is whether he can manage to get up on his feet and stay there long enough to express his thanks. I have, as you see, achieved the first part of this exercise; and the length of my speech will depend on how far I can carry out the second part. I can safely promise you that my subsidence will not be delayed for very long.

To thank you for your magnificent hospitality would be hard enough by itself, but you have made my task even harder. You have actually thanked us for coming here and enjoying that hospitality. You have even gone so far as to drink our health, after you have done everything you could to undermine it. I can think of only one reply to your generous toast. Whatever difficulties we are going to have in getting home, we had none in getting here. There was absolutely no inconvenience to any of us. If we really earned your thanks by coming here—and it seems very difficult to to believe—then we are quite ready to confer the same favour again, as many times as you like!

Gentlemen, on behalf of the guests I offer you my warmest thanks for this most enjoyable evening.

38. ABSENT FRIENDS.

This speech should be short and sincere. Humour is best avoided, as flippancy would be in bad taste.

Specimen

Ladies and gentlemen, you do not want a long speech to introduce this toast. It is a simple toast with a wealth of meaning. Most of us have family and friends a long way away, whom we wish were with us now. Their presence would add to the enjoyment of our festivities. But I am sure that they would want us to enjoy ourselves just as much in their absence, and would ask no more than that we should make a brief pause to think of them for a few moments, and drink in silence to—Absent friends.

39. A Birthday Toast.

The character of this speech will naturally depend greatly on the age of the person whose birthday is being celebrated. The toast is usually proposed by an old friend, and he is allowed to relate some humorous anecdotes drawn from the friendship. While the proposer will naturally point out some of the good qualities of his friend, he should avoid fulsome praise or he will cause embarrassment and may appear insincere.

Specimen

Ladies and gentlemen, I have been asked to propose this toast because I am —— oldest friend. I am not sure if this does him justice. An old saying tells us that a man should be judged by the choice of his friends, and I should hate to think that ——'s reputation was linked too closely to mine. I think I can say that it is only in this matter of choosing friends that I have better taste than he has.

It is not merely for his good taste that —— deserves our good wishes. I am not going to embarrass him by reciting a catalogue of his many fine qualities, but I think he will forgive me if I tell you of just one little experience that we shared many years ago. (Describe an incident to the credit of the subject of the toast.)

So, ladies and gentlemen, I ask you to join me in drinking

F

the health of —— —— and in wishing him many happy
returns of his birthday. May he have many more birthdays
to come!

40. REPLY TO A BIRTHDAY TOAST.

Ladies and gentlemen, —— —— (name of proposer)
has done me many acts of friendship in the past, and I have
always appreciated them; but to-day, I think, he has been
much too kind and not very truthful. He has credited me
with virtues I have never possessed and conveniently forgotten all my failings. I am not going to correct him, because
if I did you would start doubting whether any friend of
mine could be as fine a man as you know —— to be. The
fact is that I am lucky in my friends, and the proof of my
good fortune is in the company that has honoured me by
coming here today. No-one could ask for a finer birthday
present than the company I see before me tonight. Ladies
and gentlemen, thank you very much for your kind wishes.

41. COMING OF AGE (MAN).

Ladies and gentlemen, it is my very pleasant duty to
propose the health of —— on reaching his majority. I will
not use the expression "coming of age" for, frankly, I dis-
like it. If age comes at twenty-one, then I must have died
years ago. And how can you think of age when you look at
—— to me he represents the coming of youth. He is old
enough in the sense that he has now reached the age when
most people stop wanting to be older. Happily he has a
good many years to enjoy before he will reach the age when
he will start to want to be younger.

Some people never grow up and others are old for their
age; I hope —— will take it as a compliment when I express
the opinion that he seems to me to be absolutely twenty-one
in every respect. I am not going to embarrass him by reciting
a catalogue of his many fine qualities, nor am I going to
bore him with the advice of an older man which he would

probably ignore anyway. I think it was Somerset Maughan who said that there is a sort of conspiracy among older folks to pretend that they are wiser than younger folks, and the younger folks do not rumble it until they themselves have grown older—and then, of course, it pays them to join in the conspiracy, so that it goes on for ever.

I am sure that —— will live a happy, successful and useful life for he has all the qualities necessary for this enviable trinity. So, ladies and gentlemen, I give you this toast. To our good friend —— ——.

42. REPLY TO A COMING OF AGE TOAST (MAN).

Ladies and gentlemen, I have heard it said that young men think older men are fools, and that older men *know* young men to be so. One day I shall learn how far true the second part of the saying is; I hope it is not entirely accurate, for I can say quite honestly that I do not hold with the first part. For the moment I must express my thanks for the honour you have paid me on this rather important occasion to myself. I must also thank you very much for not asking how it feels to be twenty-one, for of course, it feels just the same as being twenty.

I am not going to attempt to reply to the compliments you have paid me, which are entirely undeserved; but I feel bound to say one thing. Whatever advantages I have in life I owe entirely to my mother and father. If I succeed in anything, it is thanks largely to them; if I fail, the fault lies with myself. If I can live up to their standards I shall think myself a lucky man. Once again, thank you very much.

43. AT A COMING OF AGE (WOMAN).

Specimen

Ladies and gentlemen, My task tonight is an honour rather than a duty, for I am sure that I am generally envied for being chosen to propose the health of ———— on her twenty-first birthday. My only qualification is that I have had the privilege of wishing her many happy returns on most of her other birthdays. I can even remember her first birthday when I took her in my arms, and later occasions when she sat on my knee. You will, I am sure, appreciate that I recall these things rather wistfully, for I am unlikely to get any further opportunities of this nature.

I have watched ———— grow up. I have seen childish prettiness give way to womanly beauty; I have seen good nature broaden into charm. To me she has always been sweet and lovable and I am sure she will remain the same for the rest of her life.

Ladies and gentlemen, I ask you to join me in drinking the health of ———— and wishing her many happy returns of her birthday.

44. REPLY TO A COMING OF AGE TOAST (WOMAN).

No formal speech is required. All that the lady is expected to do is get up and voice her thanks in her own words.

Specimen

Ladies and gentlemen, Please don't ask me for a speech. I am very happy and proud to receive your good wishes, and I find it all so exciting that I don't know how to say all I think. Just one thing I can say, and mean, with all my heart—thank you all, so very much!

45. A WEDDING ANNIVERSARY TOAST.

This is a specimen of a speech given at a Dinner to celebrate a Silver Wedding, but it can be adapted to suit any anniversary.

Specimen

Ladies and gentlemen, I can almost say that I have looked

forward to this moment for twenty-five years, for I was
present at the wedding of the charming couple in whose
honour I am speaking tonight. It is sometimes said that a
friend who marries is a friend lost; but when ———— got
married, I not only retained his friendship, but gained
another friend too. For twenty-five years I have enjoyed the
kindness of our host and hostess, and if I can enjoy the same
friendship until their wedding turns from silver to gold,
then I shall be very happy.

It is, I think, just as well that I am here tonight to vouch
for the authenticity of the celebration. Had I not had the
proof of my own eyes, I should find it hard to believe that
our host and hostess have been married so long. In looks
and spirit they are both so much younger than their years;
and their obvious delight in each other could not be sur-
passed by newly weds. I think I can say that their honey-
moon has lasted for twenty-five years, and looks like lasting
the rest of their lives.

Let us drink to their health and wish them as much
happiness together in the future as they have had in the
past. They could not have more. Ladies and gentlemen,
to Mr. and Mrs. ————.

46. Reply to a Wedding Anniversary Toast.

Specimen

Ladies and gentlemen, I have been looking forward to the
opportunity of expressing the thanks of my wife and myself
for your kind wishes and many charming gifts to mark this
occasion in our married life. Now you have placed us further
in your debt by your most generous response to this toast,
and made my task more difficult than ever. Indeed, I can
recall only one other occasion in my life when I had to get
up and try to express feelings that could not be done full
justice by any words. That occasion, of course, was exactly
twenty-five years ago today. All I could manage to stammer

out then was that I thought I was the luckiest man in the world; and all I can stammer out now is that I know I am the luckiest man in the world.

For twenty-five years I have enjoyed life with the perfect wife, while she has suffered a husband imperfect in all save one thing: his love for her. We have been happy together and I think we should have been happy on a desert island; but we have not lived apart from the world and a good deal of our mutual happiness has been brought to us by common friends. Tonight those friends are with us. And so we thank you all, not only for your kind wishes and presents, but for the joys you have given us since we were married.

47. THE SPIRIT OF CHRISTMAS.

Speeches are not usual at a family Christmas Dinner, but where such a function includes friends as well as relatives, a formal proposal of this toast may be desired. The note should be, of course, on a cheerful and convivial tone.

Specimen

Ladies and gentlemen, Christmas as you all know is the festival for young children. It is for their sake that we decorate our homes with holly and mistletoe. It is for their sake that we put on paper hats and play jolly games. It is for their sake that we eat turkey and Christmas pudding and a whole variety of other good things. It is for their sake alone—or so we say; and if you believe that, you can believe it is for the sake of the children, too, that we drink port and smoke cigars on this occasion.

Please do not think I am decrying the idea that Christmas is primarily a children's feast day. On the contrary its great merit is that it makes children of us all. It is the one time in the year when we can forget our grown-up dignity and have a good time. This, I think, is the spirit of Christmas and I ask you to join me in drinking to it.

48. THE NEW YEAR'S EVE DINNER.

Specimen

Ladies and gentlemen, there is no danger of my detaining you for long, for it is almost midnight. When the clock strikes and the bells ring, I am going to ask you to drink with me to a happy and successful New Year, and to our reunion here in exactly a year's time. As we drink the toast I ask you to spare a thought for absent friends, and let us hope that next year they will be with us. Ladies and gentlemen, the hour is striking, and I give you the toast of a Happy New Year!

CHAPTER EIGHT

Sporting Toasts

49. OUR OPPONENTS.

SPORTSMANSHIP must obviously be the keynote of these toasts, with emphasis on friendly rivalry and the fact that the game is more important than the result. If your own side has won, make little of the success, mention any luck you may have had, and dwell on the difficulty your team experienced before it could claim the victory. If your side has lost, do not bemoan the absence of your best players or claim that you were unlucky; say that the better team won, and that you hope to get your revenge next time.

Often the convention is for the toast to be proposed by the captain of the winning team and answered by his opposite number; but sometime the toast is proposed by the captain of the home team, irrespective of the results of the match.

The specimen given is for a Dinner following an Annual Cricket Match, but this can obviously be adapted to suit any form of Sporting Dinner where a toast to our opponents is to be given.

Specimen

Ladies and gentlemen, I have the greatest pleasure in proposing the toast of our opponents. I know you will agree with me that we had an excellent game. As it happened, we managed to scrape a win, and on paper it may look a comfortable victory. In fact, as you all know, our opponents gave us some very uncomfortable moments, and the score-book flatters us. Of course I am glad we won; but I am happier still that we had such a good game. Our opponents were not only keen and able players—their fielding in particular, was a lesson to us—but they showed themselves fine sportsmen. It is not for the result that we shall remember this game so much as the spirit in which it was played. The next time we meet we shall try to win again, although I don't mind admitting that we expect at least as hard a struggle as we had today, but whatever the result we know in advance that we shall have a good game, played in the spirit in which cricket should always be played.

Gentlemen, I give you the toast of our opponents, the ———— (name of club), coupled with the name of their Captain, ————.

50. REPLY TO THE TOAST OF OUR OPPONENTS.

Ladies and gentlemen, on behalf of a very chastened team, I wish to thank you for your most cordial toast. We have been soundly beaten, and I had no intention to try to make excuses; but I did not expect to hear excuses made for us. You are too generous in your victory and I can only reply by saying that the better team won, and we know it. But it is a great comfort to hear that you do not consider your afternoon was entirely wasted, or that you might have done better at the nets. Whatever faults there were in our play—and I know there were plenty—we tried our hardest to give you a good game. The simple fact was that you were too good for us. But we enjoyed the match tremendously, and it is a relief to hear that you got some pleasure out of it.

I must thank you also for the way in which you have entertained us. This afternoon you provided us with an excellent tea, and tonight we have enjoyed this magnificent dinner, which I feel we have done very little to deserve.

According to my memory, a fixture has been arranged for a return match on our ground in six weeks' time. Then we shall have the pleasure of offering you hospitality—which I am afraid will hardly match yours—and, we hope, of avenging today's defeat. It may seem boastful to make this suggestion after our performance today; but like most cricketers we never know when we are beaten, and the next time we take the field against you we shall be more determined than ever. Anyway whatever the result, I share your knowledge that we are going to have another good, sporting game.

On behalf of the ———— Club, I thank you.

51. THE TEAMS.

Sometimes the toast of both teams together is proposed, and this is especially agreeable when there has been a big margin of victory. The following specimen can be used for any team sport.

Specimen

Ladies and gentlemen, it gives me very great pleasure to propose the toast of the two teams who have entertained us so well this afternoon. I think everyone who saw the match will agree that it was a splendid game. Of course one team won, and the other lost; but I think the winners will forgive me if I say that, although they deserve our congratulations for their very fine performance, the result was not the most important part of the afternoon's entertainment. What pleased me most, and I think I am speaking for all the spectators, was the fine spirit in which the game was played. It was hard-fought yet always in the highest sporting tradition. The winners never relaxed until the game was over, and the losers gallantly carried the struggle on right up to the end.

It is not my place to single out individual players on either side, and in any case I think this would give a false idea of the match. Both teams played as teams, and the outstanding feature of the game was the high quality of the teamwork on both sides. Yet two players, I think, deserve just a word of special mention. I refer, of course, to the two captains. Each played a capital game, and each gave his side fine leadership.

Now, ladies and gentlemen, I ask you to drink to the health of the two teams and their captains ———— and ————.

52. THE CLUB.

This is the common toast at the annual club dinner and is generally proposed by the chairman. The speech should include tributes to the secretary (who will reply to the toast) and other officials, and also to the captain; but unless there has been an exceptionally outstanding player, it is advisable not to single our individual members of the team for special mention, for obvious reasons. However, any success by a club member in competitions, or in representative or other such matches should be mentioned.

Specimen

Ladies and gentlemen, it is my happy duty to rise and remind you of the success the club has enjoyed during the season that has just ended and to ask you to join me in drinking to continued success in the future.

You do not want me to review our achievements this season. They have already been placed on the record and we can feel justly proud of them. Our first eleven has won twelve matches and lost only two ; and of the six matches that were drawn, we may fairly say that the weather robbed us of victory at least three times. But I think we have little cause for complaint about the weather this season. It has not been a good summer—English summers rarely are— but a kind Providence has saved most of the rain for week-days and most of the sun for week-ends.

I know you will all support me when I pay tribute to the work of our most energetic secretary and the other officials who have given so freely of their time to make the season the success it has been. It would be invidious if I were to single out any members of the team for special mention, because our victories have been won more by teamwork than anything else, and every man has played his part. But I do not think anyone will object when I remind you of the splendid example set by our captain ————— who has excelled not only as a fine all rounder, but also in the sort of leadership that cricket needs. He has been an inspiration to the team. I must also mention the success of one of our younger players ————— in being chosen to play as an amateur for the County. As you all know, ————— has now signed professional forms with the County and next season he will be lost to us. Of course we shall miss him seriously; but we shall take pride in his future career and we wish him all the success he deserves.

Our second eleven has enjoyed less success in actual matches, but its prospects for the future are bright. There has been a welcome influx of young players into the club, and several youngsters have shown in their first season that they will soon be clamouring for places in the first eleven.

You have already seen the report of the club's financial position, and will have observed no doubt with relief—that we are still solvent. We never want to be much more, but a little extra cash in hand is necessary if we are to keep up our present standard of equipment. As a result of increased costs we have been obliged to raise the subscription of honorary members from —— to ——. No one wants to raise the subscription for playing members; and it is because we are anxious to avoid this that I am taking the liberty of reminding you that the nominal honorary subscription is a minimum sum and any individual additions to it will be most gratefully received.

Cricket is an old English game. It is essentially English

and it is by far the oldest of our popular sports. But let us not forget that it was played first—I might almost say invented—by boys. Young lads were wielding home-made bats in the days of Queen Elizabeth, when their elders looked down on the sport as a childish pastime. Now, of course, it is the sport for men of all ages. We ourselves should be hard put to it if we had to manage without our veterans; but let us remember that cricket is also the game for youth. Ours is quite an old club, but it is young in spirit. As I have said we have some very promising young players; but we need more, and it is up to us older members to do our best to attract youngsters to join us.

Now gentlemen, I ask you to join with me in drinking to the future success of the club, and with this toast I couple the name of our Honorary Secretary ————— —————.

53. REPLY TO THE TOAST OF THE CLUB.
   (Usually given by the Hon. Secretary).

Specimen

Ladies and gentlemen, Much as I appreciate the honour you have paid me in coupling my name with this toast, I feel unable to accept your compliment on my own behalf alone. On occasions like this the secretary gets all the credit; but in fact this secretary deserves very little of it. The success and smooth running of the club during the season that has just ended were due to the work of the Committee of which I am only one member. Teamwork brought the club its success on the field of play; and teamwork also was responsible for the efficient way in which the club has been run off the field.

I must hasten to assure you that I am not trying to shift the blame for my own shortcomings on to the Committee. I do not suggest that it was teamwork that caused the unfortunate misunderstanding at Easter, when we arrived at our opponents' ground at just about the same time as they arrived at ours. That was not the fault of the committee. The blame was all mine, although I can pass a little on to the Postmaster General for really the line was bad. On several other occasions the club had to suffer from my sins of omission and commission and I must tell you that in every case the Committee was quite blameless. For the things that went smoothly they deserve your praise, for the tragedies and disasters, blame me.

I should like to add my personal support to the Chairman's praise of our captain. ————— ————— is not only a fine player and a fine leader; he is also a fine coach. I have seen him at the nets, putting the youngsters through their paces, and I have seen him giving fielding practice to the team. I have no doubt that the improvement in our standard of match play owes a tremendous amount to the work put in by our captain in coaching and practice.

In thanking you once again, therefore, I ask you to rise again and drink to the health of our captain ————— —————. May he have a very long innings.

54. Reply to the Toast of the Captain.

Specimen

Ladies and gentlemen, Thank you for your kindness. It should be easy for me to reply to this toast, for I have only to tell you the truth about the way our team has pulled together and the little that has been required by the captain. Unfortunately, with a rather blatant disregard for the truth, my friend the secretary has anticipated this reply, twisted it to suit his own purpose and modestly sheltered behind it in an attempt to prove that his job was equally simple. I am sure you have not been fooled; and I am sure that the other members of our hard-working Committee will agree with me when I say that the club owes more to its secretary than to any other member.

I am not so modest as the secretary and I am going to say

quite brazenly that in one respect, at least, I think I have carried out my duties of captain extraordinarily well. I must make this boast because, quite unaccountably, neither you Mr. Chairman, nor the secretary has even bothered to mention this most important triumph of mine. As you know, we have played twenty matches during the season; and I, as captain, have won the toss no less than fifteen times! This I submit is a proud record. It is the best thing I have done for the club. And I would remind you that I did it all off my own bat. It was a personal achievement that owed nothing to teamwork.

Still, I am afraid it has been my only personal achievement. Teamwork has done all the rest. I can only say it has been a great honour to me to captain such a team, which deserves our most hearty congratulations. Thank you all.

55. THE CHAMPION.

Most clubs have their own individual championships, and at the Sports Club Dinner, he or she is usually the subject of a toast. This speech should be frankly in praise of the winner of the championship prize. Humour is essential and the introduction of a good sporting story that has not been all round the club room will be appreciated.

Specimen

Ladies and gentlemen, I am very happy to propose the health of the winner of the ————— Cup, because only a week ago he was my companion in adversity. Actually he was my opponent; but we happened to share the same bunker. I am not going to pretend that our comradeship lasted for long. Mr. ————— deserted me with quite unseemly haste, and I was left to continue the excavations by myself. After the game—and I shall not tell you the result—he expressed his entire agreement with me that the bunker in question—and I am sure you all know which one I mean—ought to be removed.

Whenever I see this bunker I am reminded of the famous cartoon which appeared in Punch shortly before the last war. It showed Benito Mussolini, the Italian Dictator, on a golf course confronted by an enormous bunker. Fixing his caddie with a stern eye he is saying "Remove that bunker!"

The moral, I suppose, is that golf is no game for dictators. It makes you modest. But I do not think Mr. ———— needed to take up golf to acquire modesty. He was born modest, and his behaviour after carrying off the ———— Cup has been most apologetic. He has even been heard to say that it was a fluke. All of you who have seen him play, and those of you who have had the chastening experience of playing against him will, I know, deny that suggestion indignantly. He was a worthy winner and he thoroughly deserved his success. Ladies and gentlemen, the champion!

56. REPLY TO THE TOAST OF THE CHAMPION.

Specimen

Ladies and gentlemen, I feel greatly honoured by your kind reception of this toast. I do not deserve it, any more than I deserve the prize that I happen to have won. There are many here tonight who play a better game than I do.

If it is possible, I am even worse at speaking than I am at playing. I have had my attack of nerves when addressing a ball, but they were nothing compared with my feelings on addressing you now. So I am going to try to hole out in one, and just tell you a little story and then sit down.

(Here insert a suitable humorous story).

And with that, ladies and gentlemen, I ask you to excuse me. Again, many thanks for your kind toast.

57. THE ANGLING CLUB.

Anglers are proverbially tellers of tall stories and the speaker should not hesitate to tell a tall one on this occasion.

Specimen

Ladies and gentlemen, After skilfully avoiding the bait for many years I have at last been hooked. No doubt your chairman, who did the angling is very pleased with himself. He has landed his victim and for better or worse the task of proposing this toast is mine. Personally I am sure it could not have been worse; and the chairman is going to find that he made a very poor catch indeed. And, it is too late to throw it back now!

The trouble is that I have no idea what to say. I could say that I hope you will all have great success with your angling and land many large fish; but if I did I should not be telling the truth. Who ever heard of an angler hoping that all the big fish nibbled his rivals' baits? Then again, I could tell you a tall story—but you wouldn't believe it. So I am going to tell you instead a very simple tale which you will have no difficulty in swallowing. (Here follow with a very tall tale).

Anglers have a reputation for jollity. There are pubs scattered all over the country called "The Jolly Angler". You have never seen an inn called "The Gloomy Angler". Yet I doubt if we look very jolly types when we are angling. The explanation, I think, must be that after long periods of enforced silence and patience, we become jolly by way of reaction when we go and slake our thirst. It is fit and proper that we are meeting now in an inn, and I think you have had enough enforced silence and patience while I have been on my feet. So, here's to jollity and—Success to Angling!

58. THE ROWING CLUB.

Ladies and gentlemen, Before I ask you to drink to the success of the Club, I must beg you to approve an expression of thanks to two persons. One is our secretary, who not only organised everything with great success throughout the season, but who also arranged this excellent dinner we have just had. The other person to whom we are indebted is the

G

Clerk of the Weather, who gave us some bad breaks at times, but smiled at us in the end.

I am not going to repeat the results of the various events in which we have competed, because you know them already. We have by no means disgraced ourselves, and I am sure that our standard will be at least as high next year.

The object of rowing is, of course, to win the race. But it is the race rather than the victory that counts most, and collecting trophies has its limitations as a pastime. We believe that rowing is a grand sport. I am not trying to underrate the importance of the competitive element, but I do think you will agree when I say that it is the competition itself rather than the result that gives the greatest pleasure.

So, ladies and gentlemen, when I ask you to drink to our future success, I should like to think of that word "success" in its broadest sense. So, raise your glasses, if you please, and let us drink the toast—Success to the Club.

CHAPTER NINE

After Dinner Stories and Jokes

THIS chapter represents a miscellany of humorous stories and anecdotes, many of which can be adapted to suit special circumstances and bring in personalities who are present at the Dinner. In choosing any particular joke for retelling at a function, the first consideration should be as to suitability. Firstly is it in good taste, bearing in mind the type of audience to be present; secondly does it have any connection with the main body of the speech. If the answer to both these questions is yes, then an additional interest will be added to your speech, if the story is told. Otherwise, leave well alone and save your favourite funny story for another occasion.

When telling these stories try not to copy them word for word; vary the retelling to suit your style of delivery. One final word of warning. If any particular story has already gone the rounds of your club, or association, it is better not to use it at all; find another story that is likely to have fresh appeal, or omit it entirely from your speech.

STRICTLY STAG.

A very attractive, although rather naïve, young lady had the misfortune to develop a bad cold the very night she was due to attend a fashionable dinner dance. Having no wish to miss the event, she wisely took the precaution of having two very large handkerchiefs with her. In common with most members of the female sex, her handbag was far too small to hold both handkerchiefs together with all the other items which fill a lady's handbag, and so she put one in the bag, and the other into the top of her rather low cut evening gown. During the course of the dinner—and the usual rather long, dull speeches which followed—she had to resort to the handkerchief in the handbag on more than one occasion. Eventually it became unuseable, but her nose continued to trouble her. Choking back yet another sneeze, she reached hurriedly into the top of her gown for the emergency handkerchief. Unfortunately, however, her movements during dinner had caused the handkerchief to change position and she could not find it. Her hand explored a little to this side and then that. Still no handkerchief. Becoming desperate she plunged deeper, and at that precise moment noticed the amused eyes of the young man opposite fixed on her. She blushed and feeling some explanation was due, she sought desperately for words to explain the situation. Blushing still deeper, she finally managed to blurt out—"I was sure I had two when I came out."

A well-known solicitor had been called upon to defend a young lady who had been up for trial on alleged offences under the new Act. Owing to his eloquence and legal skill the young woman—a somewhat improbable blonde—was acquitted and was consequently very grateful to her legal representative.

Some few weeks after the trial, while walking out for an evening stroll with his wife, the solicitor noticed his blonde client walking on the opposite side of the road. The client waved to him effusively, and greeted him with perhaps rather more warmth than the circumstances warranted. As they passed out of earshot, the solicitor's wife looked suspiciously at her husband. "And where did you meet that hussy?" she asked. Her husband, feeling a little uncomfortable stammered and stuttered for a bit, finally blurted out "Oh—er—just professionally, my dear." Replied the wife "Hers or yours?"

The new school inspector was very young and rather apt to become easily flustered. Came the day when he found himself having to address a class of fifteen year old boys, all due to leave school at the end of the term. Hesitatingly, he tried to explain to them about life in the grown up world; now that they were now young men and children no longer, and how they must take on the responsibilities of citizenship. Not wishing to paint too gloomy a picture, he said that they would find that working life had its compensations. "Indeed," he elaborated "Every age has its compensations—childhood, schooldays. You boy," he pointed to a boy in the front row. "You enjoyed your infancy didn't you?" The boy had not the faintest idea what the inspector was talking about, but true to school training he answered smartly "Oh, yes, sir." "Well then, that's what I mean" the inspector continued rapidly. "Just as, when an infant, you enjoyed your infancy, so as an adult, you will find you enjoy your adultery."

In the vicarage garden there was a sudden scuffle in the hen house. Out of the run, and over the wire netting came a small black-and-white hen pursued vigorously by a raucous, long legged rooster. Half running, half flying the little hen darted out of the garden into the main road. A passing lorry hit her and that, alas, was that.

From the vicarage window, the two elderly spinsters watched the proceedings with approval. Finally, one turned to the other "You see, Emily," she said "she'd rather die."

The village spinster called into the local police station and complained to the village constable that some of the young men of the village were bathing in the river outside her house, completely nude. The constable promised to take action.

A few days later, she was back. "Haven't they moved," said the constable, "I told them to". "Well, yes, they've moved," she said, "but they are still visible from my bedroom window." The P.C. sighed. "All right, madam, I'll see to it."

The next day she was back yet again. "Oh, come now, madam," the constable reproved. "I am sure you cannot see the boys from your bedroom window now." "No," she agreed, the view from her bedroom window was uninterrupted as far as she could see. "But," she added, "If I go up into the attic and use the field glasses, I can still see them."

An artist celebrated for his artistic studies of the female nude arrived at the studio one morning with a dilly of a hangover. His model started to disrobe, but the artist stopped her. "Keep your clothes on, for a while," he said, "I'm not ready to start working yet; I must have some coffee and aspirins." The sympathetic model taking in at a glance his unhappy state, generously offered to make the coffee for him, which offer the artist accepted with relief.

The coffee having been made, the two were just sitting down to drink it, when familiar footsteps were heard ascending the staircase. The artist leaped to his feet. "Goodness," he exclaimed. "That's my wife. She mustn't see us like this. Quick Miss Jones, get your clothes off."

Young Harry was a very fine swimmer and spent much of his time at the local swimming baths. Unfortunately, his wife did not care very much for the sport and rarely accompanied her husband. However, while at the pool Harry struck up an acquaintance with a young woman who had been amply endowed by nature with all the more obvious feminine charms.

One day, when sitting in a bus with his wife, who should board the vehicle but the attractive young woman in question. Ever polite, Harry bid her "Good morning," and was rather surprised to receive a haughty toss of the head in return. Feeling upset, Harry sat back in his seat and made no further effort to pursue the conversation.

Finally, the attractive lady reached her destination and as she got to her feet, she looked icily at Harry once more. Then recognition dawned. "Oh," she gasped, "I am so sorry. It is Harry, isn't it. I am afraid I just didn't recognise you with your clothes on."

The two friends were having a round of golf. It was a peculiarity of this pair that one was very long-sighted, while the other was short-sighted in the extreme. As they reached the ninth hole and the short-sighted one was about to drive off, his friend stopped him. "Wait a bit, old man," he cautioned, "Can't you see those two women playing the hole?" The short-sighted one shook his head, but prepared to wait patiently. However after a few minutes, it became apparent to the long sighted player that the women had finished the hole and were just standing there talking. In the time honoured fashion "Fore!" he shouted. "Fore," he yelled again at the top of his voice. Unfortunately, the ladies either couldn't or wouldn't hear him. "Look, old boy," he addressed his companion, "could you go over there and tell them to move". "Well, why don't you go," immediately replied the friend. "Its like this," the long sighted golfer explained, in a rather embarrassed way. "One of those women is my wife and the other is—well, I suppose you'd call her 'a friend'." "I see" the short-sighted fellow nodded sympathetically, and walked across the green towards the two offending females. Within a few yards of them, however, he stopped abruptly, and rushed back to his partner, his face red with more than exertion. "Small world, isn't it," he stammered.

SHAGGY DOGS.

A man entered the doctor's surgery. Blood was pouring down his face. The doctor examined him and found a nasty gash on his right ear. "How did this happen?" asked the doctor. "I bit myself," came the laconic reply. The doctor frowned. "Don't be ridiculous," he said. "How can a man bite himself on his own ear?" Replied the patient simply. "Well, I had to stand on a chair, of course doctor."

Johnnie walked into the little country pub and was astonished to see a man sitting down at a draught-board, with a dog as his playing companion. Each player had three pieces on the board. The man moved putting one of his pieces into obvious jeopardy. The dog pounced and "huffed" the piece. Too late, he perceived his error, as the man then proceeded to "huff" the dog's remaining three pieces in one move.

Johnnie was staggered. Walking up to the man he commented. "That's a fantastically clever dog, you have there." "Oh, I don't know," answered the man "I wouldn't say that. I can always beat him."

He was homeward bound, minding his own business and walking quietly along the sidewalk. Suddenly the horse spoke to him. It was an ordinary kind of horse, the kind which used to draw milk-carts through all our cities, and he was the last one of his breed still plying his old trade. The man stopped, stared incredulously at the horse. "Did you say something," he asked. The horse snorted "Of course I said something. I said did you know I once won the Derby?" At this moment the milkman came along the street. The passer-by stopped him and said. "You won't believe this, but your horse just spoke to me." "Oh, yes," the milkman was plainly unbelieving. "And I suppose he told you he once won the Derby." "That's right," the passer-by was excited. "Well he's a flaming liar, that horse," said his owner. "In point of fact, he only came third."

The two frogs had had a heavy night of it, and the grandfather of all hangovers was their morning reward. "We need some aspirins," said one. The other agreed, but he felt too ill to walk down to the village to get them. "I know," the first one had an inspiration. "We'll send Sammy Snail." He called the snail over, gave him half-a-crown and told him to get a big bottle of aspirin. Six months later, they were still waiting.

"Sammy has been a long time gone," said the second frog. "You don't suppose the little blighter has done a bunk with your money?" From a clump of grass, a few feet away a tiny voice was raised. "If you two stinkers don't stop talking about me like that behind my back, I shan't go at all!"

The visiting Cricket team had arrived. Ten men and a horse. The home side had plenty of humorous things to say about this. But to their astonishment when the visiting side went out to bat, the horse was trotted out to the wicket as their number one batsman. Scornfully, the home side's bowler started his first over. Scorn turned to amazement however, as over after over, the horse stayed at the wicket, knocking fours, sixes, and defying the entire bowling might of the home side to get him out. At the end of the match, the visitors had knocked a mighty 150, with the horse carrying his bat for 138.

The home captain was a bit nettled by this. "I suppose," he said nastily to the visiting captain. "That now that horse of yours is going to amaze us all by his bowling ability." The visiting skipper looked at the home captain with a superior smirk. "Now, don't be ridiculous, old man," he answered. "Who on earth has ever heard of a horse who could bowl?"

He was a theatrical agent of some standing. He was also bored. There were no new acts, these days. He'd seen them all, heard them all, and booked them all. Unless something really startling came his way, he was going to retire and keep pigs.

Then one day into his office walked a man with a great Dane and a tiny poodle. Without any explanation the great Dane suddenly launched into a spirited rendering of "One Fine Day." The agent yawned. "Performing dog," he growled. "Seen plenty of them in my time, nothing new in that." The dogs' owner explained. "Perhaps I ought to tell you it's a trick." The agent's boredom lifted a little. "Well, that might be different," he commented. "What's the trick?" "You see," the little man confided. "The great Dane can't sing a note really, but the poodle's a smashing ventriloquist."

For Sportsmen

The village batsman tipped the ball beautifully and there was a chance of a quick single. A fraction of a second before the batsman reached the wicket at the other end, a well aimed ball had dislodged the middle stump. "How's that," roared the fielder, the whole of the visiting team, and the spectators. "Not out" was the majestic reply from the umpire.

The batsman smiled gratefully at the umpire, who happened also to be the village barber. "That was a close shave," he commented facetiously. "Yes, it was," agreed the umpire, "And if you were not a regular customer, it would have been a case of next gentleman, please."

In the pavilion, the telephone rang. The secretary took the call.

"Why, good morning, Mrs. Binks. I am afraid your husband has just gone out to bat. Shall I ask him to ring you back later?"

"No, don't bother," came the reply from the other end. "I'll just hold the line."

His lordship and a party of house guests decided to have a friendly cricket match in the grounds of the stately home. The second footman was called upon to umpire.

While batting, his lordship was guilty of an obvious l.b.w. "How's that?" the bowler asked in gentlemanly tones. The footman stood woodenly to attention, his eyes fixed on some distant object. "His lordship," he announced in stately fashion, "Is not at home."

"What kind of ruling is that?" asked his noble employer with some indignation.

"In plain words, my lord" the footman descended to humanity again. "You're out."

The keen cricketer had taken his newest fancy to see the local cricket match. Although undeniably blessed by nature with all feminine appeal, the young woman was clearly in the back row when brains and intelligence were handed out. All through the afternoon, the young man had tried to explain the finer points of the game to his unresponsive companion, who giggled feebly and inanely at such terms as "Three slips and one short leg" and "third man" (there were clearly 13 men on the field, not counting the referees in their white coats!)

Finally, after a spectacular piece of bowling, she asked her companion. "Why did you say that he had done the hat-trick?" "You see," answered the exasperated cricketer. "It was done by a bowler."

The local reporter, after an afternoon watching a more than usually dull cricket match, turned in this piece of "copy" to his editor.

"We have never witnessed a match in which the fielders suffered so much from buttered fingers. Time after time the balls were skied and ought to have been caught, but were not caught. There was, in fact, a non-catching epidemic."

The referee's whistle went. "Free kick there" he shouted importantly. "For whom?" asked the home captain. This flustered the referee. "Us," he answered wildly.

"Who's Tom Smith?" asked the curious man in the local pub. "Tom Smith?" replied the local. "Why don't you know, he's the man who saved us from defeat in the football match, last Saturday."

"Really," the visitor was interested. "What position does he play then?".

The local smiled knowingly. "In a manner of speaking, he don't play at all. He's the ref."

They had lost their match, and in a reproachful mood they were travelling home together. "It wasn't my fault," said the first. "If you chaps moved faster, we could have beaten them easily." "Move faster," refuted the second player indignantly. "I'll have you know that only last week I won the half-mile event at the athletics meeting. I got a gold medal, too, to prove it. It's Jones fault we lost. He can't kick a football for love or money."

The third player lost his temper. "Can't kick a football is it? Well I've kicked the ball for one mile with one kick, and I've got a medal to prove it. It's Sproggins whose to blame, he just ain't no footballer."

Sproggins spoke loud in his own defence. "Oh, yes I am" he maintained stoutly. "You fellers and your one medal make me sick. Why I've got six gold medals, thirteen silver cups, two presentation sets of carvers, and fourteen plaques." "We know that," the first man spoke again. "But the judge called it housebreaking."

The county match was under way. One of the players was

obviously new and very nervous. His opponent drove off hitting the ball mightily so that it dropped neatly on the green a few inches away from the hole.

The newcomer was more frightened than ever. "Does he always do that," he whispered to the caddie. "Oh, no," came the cheerful reply. "Didn't you notice? His foot slipped."

The golfing father had decided to take his family down to the golf club, so that they could watch his prowess in the championship. Unfortunately it was one of those days well known to golfers when success was determined to elude him.

After following father from hole to hole, and watching his game with great interest, the little girl suddenly demanded of her mother in an ear-piercing voice audible to everyone around. "Mummy, why isn't Daddy allowed to knock his ball into that little tin pot?"

The new member decided he knew it all. He declined the services of the professional, and made his lordly way out on to the course. He teed up, drove mightily and the ball skimmed away over the hedge and onto the main road.

A few moments later, the professional dashed up. "Did you hit that ball over the hedge just now?" he asked. The clever one nodded. "Well," said the professional. "You may be interested to know that the ball hit a passing cyclist, knocking him off his bicycle, a bus which was following had to swerve to avoid running over the cyclist, and as a result knocked down the wall of a cottage on the corner of the road. There are now three break-down lorries, two squad cars with policemen, four St. John's Ambulance men, two A.A. scouts, and a traffic jam of two miles long in each direction."

"Goodness" said the smart golfer, paling visibly and his confidence evaporating rapidly. "What shall I do?"

The professional seized his opportunity. "Hold the club,

so," he instructed. "Now, watch your stance, head down, ..."

He stalked in through the front door, flung down his clubs in the middle of the floor, marched into the sitting room and dropped heavily into his chair.

He glared at his wife. "I'll tell you what," he growled. "I am not going to play on that Course again. The greens are ill-kept; the tees are torn to bits; trespassers will walk about the fairway as if it were a public common; the members don't know the first thing about sportsmanship, and . . ."

"What did you lose by, dear?" his wife asked sympathetically.

He was showing his fiancée how to play—and not with any marked degree of success. She had made every mistake possible, and even invented a few errors that had not been thought of before. At last, however, by a fluke she performed a neat little shot and the ball rolled out of view. He ran ahead to note its position. When he saw the ball, he turned to her and cried out "A dead stymie."

"Oh, the poor thing," she wailed. "I hope I didn't do it with that last ball."

The couple in front made very slow progress so that the two golfers who followed had to wait at nearly every green. On one occasion the front pair halted and searched in the rough. After a long wait, one of the oncoming players went up to help them in the search.

"Whereabouts do you think the ball fell?" he inquired.

"Ball," answered the novice. "Oh that's still on the tee. I'm looking for my club."

He played an atrocious game; his drives always slithered along the ground and the ball never went more than a score or so of yards. As he was making for the club-house after thoroughly boring his opponent, an inspiration came over him. "I think I've hit upon the reason for my poor play," he said brightly. "I stand too near the ball before I drive." "Well, I think," retorted his opponent. "That your trouble is that you stand too near the ball *after* you drive."

The player was one of the worst and, to add to it all, he was full of irritating little mannerisms which made the caddie justly fed-up. After missing every kind of opportunity, he arrived at a tee and went down on one knee to arrange the little heap of sand. "That's something like," yelled the caddie, "and mind you end up with 'and please make me a better player'."

First fisherman: Are these waters private?
Second fisherman: No.
First fisherman: Then it won't be a crime if I catch a fish?
Second fisherman: No, it will be a miracle.

The vicar was walking along by the river bank one Sunday afternoon and saw the local *enfent terrible* fishing. "My boy" said the reverend gentleman "Do you not know that it is wicked to fish on the sabbath?"

"Whose fishing?" queried the boy. "I'm just learning this here worm how to swim."

After a poor day's fishing some friendly anglers were sitting round the warm fire in the bar parlour. As the hour grew, the tales took on more and more enormous proportions, until at last one of the members told the story to cap all stories.

"I was once fishing in the States for—for" he hesitated.

"For whales?" suggested one of his listeners.

"No, no," snapped the other. "We were baiting the hooks with whales."

The sporting parson was making his way to church one

Sunday evening when he saw two boys fishing. He stopped. "My lads," he said. "Do you not know that this is the Sabbath, and you ought not to. . . ."

Just then one of the floats went under with a plomp. "You've got a bite; you've got a bite. Whip it up, you young slow coach," yelled the parson.

The curate was sitting on the river bank with his sister and his fiancée—both extremely attractive young ladies.

The local ne'er-do-well passed by. "Caught anything?" he enquired.

"Sir" answered the curate repressively, "I fish not for fish; I fish for human souls."

"Then, all I can say is" said the shameless one, looking at the two ladies. "You must use damned good bait."

The angler had fished all day in a large pond, where his friend had told him an enormous carp lurked.

Towards evening a farm hand came along and the disappointed angler questioned him.

"Are there any carp in this pond, can you tell me?"

"I dunno, sir, I'm sure" said the yokel.

"Well I was told that this pond, the Monastery pond, teemed with them."

"Ah, but then the Monastery pond aint here; it lies over yonder behind them bushes."

"Then what is the name of this pond?" asked the angler.

"There again, mister, I dunno. You see there was no pond 'ere two days ago. It come with Toosday's thunderstorm."

The two men met in the local. "What's your new shooting tenant like?" asked the first. "Well," replied the second. "All I can say is that he is a man of his word. He made a promise that all he shot he would send to the cottage hospital, and so far the ambulance has taken a keeper and a friend of his."

his surprise on getting inside he found the shop stacked out with salt. There were boxes of it, barrels of it, sacks of it. They littered the floor, the shelves, the counter. He asked for his cigarettes. The shopkeeper rummaged among his huge stock of salt, but failed to find any. "Must be through in the warehouse," he said. As he opened the rear door to go through to the warehouse the customer was amazed to see that the passageway behind was stacked with salt too. Intrigued he followed the shopkeeper out to the warehouse. Here, again, was ton upon ton of salt. As the shopkeeper hunted amongst all this salt for the cigarettes, the customer could not help observing: "You must sell an awful lot of salt." The shopkeeper straightened up and spread his hands in a despairing gesture. "No," he said. "I can't sell any salt. But the traveller who sells *me* salt—can *he* sell salt."

The two farm hands were having an argument and Garge, who had "discovered" the amazing new principle that all men were equals, was having great difficulty in making Willum understand the principles of his new found creed. "It's share and share alike," he said. "If you've got something someone else hasn't, then you give them half." Willum seemed to be getting the general drift of it. "I see," he said. "You mean that if you had a thousand pounds and I hadn't then you'd give I half?" Garge nodded. "That's the ticket," he said. Said Willum "And if you had two moty cars, then you'd give I one?" Again Garge nodded. Said Willum, "And if you had a pig and I hadn't, then you'd give I half?" Garge thought that one out quickly. Then he said "No ruddy fear—I've *got* a pig."

The debate in the House was in full swing, and tempers were a little frayed. Said the spokesman for one party (being very careful to use Parliamentary language) "The hon. member opposite is quite evidently suffering from an attack of beri-beri, the main sign of that disease being a swollen head." In a flash the leader of the other party was on his feet and retorting: "The hon. gentleman opposite clearly knows very little of medicine. The symptoms of beri-beri are not a swollen head, but swollen feet." Back came the reply: "It makes no difference. All I intended to convey was that you were getting rather too big for your boots."

Learned counsel was addressing a judge who was obviously extremely hostile to the cause being pleaded. Nevertheless counsel persisted in his argument which was long, involved and highly technical. The judge heard him out with no very good grace, and when he had concluded could not resist saying, sneeringly. "Mr. Prodder has spoken at great length and with a good deal of eloquence, and I know it must pain him when I say that I, for one, have been left as ignorant as ever." Quick as a flash counsel was on his feet and retorting: "Ignorant—yes, m'lud, but surely a good deal better informed."

The judge and the bishop were great friends, but loved to tease each other and indulge in a little friendly rivalry. Said the bishop: "After all, old man, you can only say to a man, 'You be hanged.' I can go much further and say to a man, 'You be damned'." The judge nodded smilingly. "Ah, yes," he said. "But the difference is that when I say to a man, 'You be hanged,' he is hanged!"

The editor of the local weekly was having an afternoon nap when into the office stormed a very peppery retired colonel complete with horse-whip which he was threatening to lay across the editor's none-too-broad shoulders. In his other hand he flourished a copy of that week's paper. "Gad sir!" he stormed. "Never been so insulted in my blasted life!" He tossed the newspaper on the desk, grabbed the editor's blue pencil and ringed the offending item. "Read that," he thundered." The editor read: "Among the other

after dinner speakers was that battle-*scared* veteran, Colonel
—" Of course, the editor apologised profusely and promised to publish an amendment in the following week's
issue. The amendment duly appeared, but did nothing to
heal the rift between the editor and the colonel. It read: "It
was, of course, a pure error that we referred to Colonel ——
last week as a battle-*scared* veteran. Everyone knows that
he could not possibly be that. On the contrary, he is what
we intended to describe him as: a *bottle*-scarred veteran.

The case being tried was one of driving while under the
influence. The policeman giving evidence, flicked the pages
of his notebook and at the very end of his recital pronounced
it as his opinion that the defendant, on the night in question,
had been "as drunk as a judge." The judge looked at him
indignantly, coughed meaningly and said: "Surely, officer,
you are mixing your metaphors a little. You mean 'as
drunk as a lord'." The policeman coloured, shuffled his
feet uncertainly and finally managed to stammer out:
"O-o-of c-c-c-course, my lord."

There was a police raid on a so called private club. In
one of the rooms at the rear of the premises they found four
men sitting round a card table. "Ha" said the police inspector, menacingly, "Caught in the act, eh? Come on, you
might as well own up—been playing cards for money
haven't you?" The first man shook his head. "Not me,
inspector, I was just having a little friendly chat." The
inspector wheeled on the second man. "Well, you were
playing anyway." Another shake of the head. "Not me,
inspector. I was just waiting for a friend." Baffled, the inspector turned to the third man. "You know very well you
were gambling." "Not me, inspector. I work here." The
fourth man got up and tried to sneak off. As he did so he
stumbled. A shower of cards and coins fell from his sleeves.
The inspector pounced on him triumphantly. "Gotya" he

said. "You've definitely been playing cards for money." The man looked at the inspector blandly. "Me playing cards, inspector? Who with?"

The new prisoner was shown into the governor's office. The governor was the type who believes in taking an interest in the men sent to him for punishment. "What are you in for?" he asked. "Forgery," said the prisoner laconically. The usual rigmarole followed. the prisoner's personal possessions being taken from him and listed before being locked in the governor's safe. The list was pushed across the desk to the prisoner and he was asked to sign it as correct. "But I can't write," he protested. The governor looked astonished. "But this is absurd," he said. "You've been sentenced for forgery and now you say that you can't write. How on earth did you get convicted?" Said the prisoner gloomily: "I reckons as 'ow I must have had a pretty rotten lawyer."

The leading man of a London amateur group was very fond of making a most theatrical entry and striking a dramatic pose which he would hold for some seconds for the benefit of the audience before getting on with his part. It was a state of affairs most irritating to some of the lesser lights, one of whom resolved to get his own back. Then they did a play in which the leading man had to enter through a couple of folding doors upstage. On the first night he made his usual style of entrance. He threw open the doors with both hands, stalked on to the stage, folded his arms and stood there impressively in the doorway. The irritated lesser light spoiled the effect entirely however, by announcing from the wings in a voice quite loud enough for the audience to hear: "Next stop—Clapham Junction."

A 'bus conductor on late shift was constantly being reprimanded by his wife for waking both her and the children when he came home in the middle of the night. He promised to mend his ways, and was as good as his word. The next night he came in very quietly, took off his shoes at the foot of the stairs and crept upstairs in his stockinged feet without making so much as a single creak. Then habit proved too much for him. He stood on the landing one hand extended, bellowing at the top of his voice: "All fez, plis."

A member of the British Legion who worked as a sorter in the local post office, was surprised to come across a letter addressed in a childish hand to "Dear God-in-heaven." He opened it, not quite knowing what else to do with it and read: "Dear God-in-heaven, I am only seven and my mother is a widow-woman. She is very pore and we haven't much to eat. Could you please send us £5." The sorter, being a decent sort, took the letter along to the Legion that night. The members had a whip-round and made up a sum of £3. 10s. They deputed one of their number to take it along to the address given in the letter. Two days later another letter addressed to "Dear God-in-heaven" arrived at the post office. The sorter opened it. It read: "Dear God-in-heaven. Thank you very much for sending mum the monie. But could you please bring it yourself next time. The British Legion chap you sent round with it kept 30s. for himself."

The charming young lady and her escort were trying to board a very full bus. Said the man as they entered the vehicle. "Can we squeeze in here, dear?" Back came the faint answer. "No, wait until we are out of the public gaze."

At the booking office. Young lady: Return, first-class, please. Clerk: Where to, Miss? Young Lady: Well, here of course, that's why I want a return.

The small boy had pestered his father with a number of questions that small boys usually do ask their fathers—

"Where", "When", "Why", "What for", and so on. Finally, he asked "Father, what do they make asphalt roads of?" Replied the father. "That's the nine-hundredth question you've asked me to-day. Do give me a little peace. What do you think would have happened to me if I had asked my father so many questions?" The boy thought about this and finally decided: "You might perhaps have learned the answers to some of my questions."

The new guest at the hotel asked the guest who was just leaving. "Why do they call this hotel the Palms? I haven't seen a single palm anywhere near the place." Replied the disillusioned departing guest. "Just you wait until you see the waiters on the day you leave."

CHAPTER TEN

Some Useful Quotations

THESE quotations should be used in moderation only, and then only if they are completely apposite to the context of the speech. The purpose of including them is rather to give some aid to the theme of a speech, than for their actual use verbatim in speech.

Nothing is more binding than the friendship of companions-in-arms.—*Hilliard.*

The commonwealth of Venice in their armoury have this inscription: Happy is that city which in time of peace thinks of war.—*Burton.*

Nothing except a battle lost can be half so melancholy as a battle won.—*Duke of Wellington.*

There never was a good war or a bad peace—*Franklin.*

War is nothing more than a reflection or image of the soul. It is the fiend within coming out.—*Channing.*

If you want to go into battle, have an Englishman at your right hand, and another at your left, and two immediately in front and two close behind. There is something in the English which seems to guarantee security. Never forget that, even when you are most irritated by the antics of these engaging madmen.—*Voltaire.*

He who loves not his country can love nothing.—*Byron.*

Danger for danger's sake is senseless.—*Leigh Hunt*.

A new recruit on putting to sea and suffering with sickness said afterwards that for the first day he was afraid he would die, and the second day he was afraid he wouldn't.—*Anon*.

Thank God, I have done my duty.—*Nelson*.

I don't know what effect these men may have on the enemy, but by Gad, they frighten me!—*Duke of Wellington (before Waterloo)*.

Never in the field of human conflict was so much owed by so many to so few.—*Winston Churchill*.

The female woman is one of the greatest institutions of which this land can boast.—*Artemus Ward*.

Great women belong to history and to self-sacrifice—*Leigh Hunt*.

Nature was in earnest when she made women—*Holmes*.

For pity is the virtue of the law and none but tyrants use it cruelly—*Shakespeare*.

The law hath not been dead, though it hath slept.—*Shakespeare*.

Fire—the most tangible of all visible mysteries.—*Leigh Hunt*.

Fire that's closest kept burns most of all.—*Shakespeare*.

Forewarned, forearmed; to be prepared is half the victory.—*Cervantes*.

Keep the home fires burning.—*Novello*.

An honest man's the noblest work of God.—*Alexander Pope*.

God often visits us, but most of the while we are not at home.—*Roux*.

To yield reverence to another, to hold ourselves and our lives at his disposal is the noblest state in which a man can live in this world.—*Ruskin*.

It is well said in every sense, that a man's religion is the chief fact with regard to him—*Carlyle*.

Religion is civilization, the highest.—*Disraeli*.

Whatever makes men good Christians makes them good citizens.—*Webster*.

He whose goodness is part of himself is what is called a real man.—*Mencius*.

I would rather have the affectionate regard of my fellow-men than I would have heaps and mines of gold.—*Dickens*.

You can only make others better by being good yourself.—*Hawers*.

We can all be angry with our neighbour. What we want is to be shown, not his defects of which we are too conscious, but his merits to which we are too blind.—*R. L. Stevenson*.

There can hardly, I believe, be imagined a more desirable pleasure than that of praise unmixed with any possibility of flattery.—*Sir Richard Steele*.

The future is purchased by the present.—*Dr. Johnson*.

A true and noble friendship shrinks not at the greatest of trials.—*Heremy Taylor*.

When men are friends, there is no need of justice; but when they are just they still need friendship.—*Aristotle*.

Sweet is the remembrance of troubles when you are in safety.—*Euripides*.

He serves his party best, who serves the country best.—*Hayes*.

There is no perfecter endowment in man than political virtue.—*Plutarch*.

Can anybody remember when times were not hard and money not scarce?—*Emerson*.

We cannot eat the fruit while the tree is in blossom.—*Disraeli*.

There's dignity in labour.—*Swain*.

Better not do the deed than weep it done.—*Prior*.

Good rarely came from good advice.—*Lord Byron*.

Advice is seldom welcome and those who want it the most always like it the least.—*Lord Chesterfield*.

Nature intended that woman should be her masterpiece.—*Lessing*.

O woman, lovely woman, nature made thee. To temper man; we had been brutes without you.—*Otway*.

I for one venerate a petticoat.—*Byron.*

The most beautiful object in the world it will be allowed is a beautiful woman.—*Macaulay.*

Man has his will; but woman has her way.—*Holmes.*

Woman will be the last thing civilized by man.—*Meredith.*

A woman is only a woman, but a good cigar is a smoke.—*Kipling.*

Absent in body, but present in spirit.—*Corinthians.*

Thy wife is a constellation of virtues; she's the moon and thou art the man in the moon.—*Congreve.*

Of all the actions of a man's life his marriage does least concern other people; yet of all actions of our life 'tis most meddled with by other people.—*Table Talk.*

No woman should marry a teetotaller or a man who does not smoke.—*R. L. Stevenson.*

The most precious possession that ever comes to a man in this world is a woman's heart.—*Holland.*

I have always thought that every woman should marry and no man.—*Disraeli.*

Every baby born into the world is a finer one than the last.—*Dickens.*

Children are the last word of human imprefections. They cry my dear; they put vexatious questions; they demand to be fed, to be washed, to be educated, to have their noses blowed; and when the time comes, they break our hearts as I break this piece of sugar.—*Stevenson.*

In general those parents have the most reverence who most deserve it.—*Dr. Johnson.*

A faithful friend is the medicine of life.—*Apochrypha.*

They are rich who have true friends.—*Fuller.*

The ornament of a house is the friends who frequent it.—*Emerson.*

A friend may well be reckoned the masterpiece of nature.—*Emerson.*

If he have not a friend, he may quit the stage.—*Bacon.*

Be slow in choosing a friend, slower in changing.—*Franklin.*

Friendship is the gift of the gods, and the most precious boon to man.—*Disraeli.*

The youth of a nation are the trustees of posterity.—*Disraeli.*

They can conquer who believe they can.—*Emerson.*

A wise man makes more opportunities than he finds.—*Bacon.*

If youth be a defect it is one that we outgrow only too soon.—*Lovell.*

Those who make the worst use of their time most complain of its shortness.—*La Bruyere.*

When the turkey's on the table and the candles on the tree; I'm jest about as happy as I ever wanta be. My children gathered round me an' my neighbours settin' by; I couldn't be no happier, and I don't wanta try.—*Carolyn Wells.*

Always play fair, and think fair; and if you win don't crow about it; and if you lose don't fret.—*Philpotts.*

Success is sweet; the sweeter if long delayed and attained through manifold struggles and defeats.—*Leigh Hunt.*

They also serve who only stand and wait.—*Milton.*

The faith they have in tennis and tall stockings, Short blistered breeches.—*Shakespeare.*

Gentlemen with broad chests and ambitious intentions do sometimes disappoint their friends by failing to carry the world before them.—*Eliot.*

There be some sports are painful, and their labour Delight in them sets off.—*Shakespeare.*

Dinna gut your fish till you get them.—*Scottish proverb.*

We may say of Angling as Dr. Boteler said of strawberries; "Doubtless God could have made a better berry, but doubt·less God never did"; and so, if I might be a judge, God never did make a more calm, quiet, innocent recreation than angling.—*Izaak Walton.*

The English winter—ending in July to recommence again in August.—*Byron.*

Work according to my feeling, is as necessary as eating and sleeping.—*Humboldt.*

Many men have been capable of doing a wise thing, many more a cunning thing, but very few a generous thing.—*Pope.*

Corporations have no souls.—*Thurlow.*

Work is the grand cure for all the maladies and miseries that ever beset mankind.—honest work.—*Carlyle.*

Man's record upon this wild world is the record of work and of work alone.—*Holland.*

No man has a right to be idle if he can get work to do, even if he be as rich as Croesus.—*Holland.*

We have a certain work to do for our bread, and that is to be done strenuously; other work for our delight, and that is to be done heartily; neither is to be done by halves or shifts.—*Ruskin.*

In all the world there is nothing so remarkable as a great man, nothing so rare, nothing so well repays study.—*Barker.*

Alcohol—liquid madness sold at 10d. the quartern.—*Carlyle.*

If abstinence on the part of a temperate drinker would reclaim any drunkard, a man of ordinary humanity would practise it as far as considerations of enjoyment were concerned.—*Bramwell.*

O thou invisible spirit of wine, if thou has not name to be known by, let us call thee devil.—*Shakespeare.*

Blessed is the man who, having nothing to say, abstains from giving us wordy evidence of the fact.—*Eliot.*

In general those who have nothing to say contrive to spend the longest time in doing it.—*Lovell.*

I am no orator as Brutus is; but as you know me all, a plain blunt man.—*Shakespeare.*

I would be loath to cast away my speech, for beside that it is excellently well penn'd, I have taken great pains to con it.—*Shakespeare.*

Do you want people to speak well of you? Then do not speak at all of yourself.—*Pascal.*

As a vessel is known by the sound, whether it be cracked

or not; so men are proved by their speeches, whether they be wise or foolish.—*Demosthenes.*

Be sure to leave other men their turns to speak.—*Bacon.*

I don't care where the water goes if it doesn't get into the wine.—*Chesterton.*

No speech ever uttered or utterable is worth comparison with silence.—*Carlyle.*

He had only one vanity; he thought he could give advice better than any other person.—*Twain.*

No fools are so troublesome as those who have some wit.—*La Rouchefoucauld.*

It is true that we are creatures of circumstances, but circumstances are also, in a great measure, the creatures of us.—*Lord Lytton.*

Remember what Simonides said—that he never repented that he had held his tongue, but often that he had spoken.—*Plutarch.*

It is a sad thing when men have neither wit to speak well nor judgment to hold their tongues.—*La Bruyere.*

Intemperance in talk makes a dreadful havoc in the heart.—*Wilson.*

The true use of speech is not so much to express our wants as to conceal them.—*Goldsmith.*